Encyclopedia of Party Ideas for Children

ENCYCLOPEDIA of PARTY IDEAS for CHILDREN

(Pre-school to Junior High)

by
LORA LEE PARROTT

ZONDERVAN PUBLISHING HOUSE
Grand Rapids, Michigan

ENCYCLOPEDIA OF PARTY IDEAS FOR CHILDREN
Copyright 1966 by
Zondervan Publishing House
Grand Rapids, Michigan

Library of Congress Catalog Card Number 65-25955

Printed in the United States of America

Contents

I. PARTY IDEAS FOR PRE-SCHOOL CHILDREN
— TWO AND THREE YEAR OLDS

1. Church House Party 9
2. Noah's Ark Party 11
3. Balloon Party 13
4. A Rainbow Party 15
5. Christmas Party 17
6. Birthday Party 19
7. Teddy Bear Party 21
8. Bible Story Hour 22
9. Valentine Party 24
10. Cowboy Party 25
11. Picnic 26
12. Other Lands Party 27
13. Playground Party 28

II. PARTY IDEAS FOR KINDERGARTEN CHILDREN
— FOUR AND FIVE YEAR OLDS

1. Snow Party 33
2. May Basket Party 34
3. Missionary Party 35
4. Bunny Hunt 37
5. Outdoor Party 39
6. Jonah and the Whale 40
7. Jack-O'-Lantern Party 41
8. Gingerbread Boy Party 43
9. Pilgrim Party 44
10. Fourth Birthday Party 46
11. Fifth Birthday Party 47
12. Bible Story Party 49
13. Promotion Day Party 50
14. Grandmothers' Tea 51
15. A Fireman's Party 52
16. Jingle Bells Christmas Party 53

III. PARTY IDEAS FOR PRIMARY CHILDREN

1. Indian Pow-Wow 57
2. Cowboy Party 59
3. Pirate Party 61
4. Doll Party 63
5. Pumpkin Party 64

6.	Easter Egg Party	66
7.	Airplane Party	68
8.	Fishing Party	70
9.	Toy Party	72
10.	Balloon Party	74
11.	Grown-up Tea Party	76
12.	Children's Christmas Party	78
13.	Spring Time Party	80
14.	Mother's Day Party	82
15.	Flag Party	84

IV. Party Ideas for Juniors

1.	A Pastor's Party	89
2.	Lincoln's Birthday Supper	90
3.	Junior Christmas Party	92
4.	Outer Space Party	94
5.	Grown-up Party	96
6.	United Nations Party	98
7.	Party for a Sick Child	100
8.	Activity Party	102
9.	Jungle Village Party	103
10.	A Welcome Party	104
11.	Junior Hallowe'en Party	106
12.	A Jiffy Party	108
13.	North Pole Party	110
14.	Hobo Party	111
15.	Father's Day Party	113
16.	Fall Round-up Party	115
17.	Indoor Party	116
18.	Junior Birthday Party	118

V. Party Ideas for Junior High Young People

1.	Sunrise Breakfast	123
2.	Junior High Hallowe'en Party	125
3.	Christmas Carol Party	128
4.	April Fool's Day Backward Party	130
5.	An All-Day Party for 'Tweenagers'	132
6.	A Candy Kitchen Party	134
7.	Indoor Picnic Party	136
8.	A Lantern Hike Party	137
9.	Doctor's Fun Clinic	138
10.	Girls' Pajama Party	140
11.	Schoolhouse Party	141
12.	A Banker's Party	143
13.	Missionary Furlough Party	145
14.	Gymnasium Party	147

Party Recipes ... 149

I. Party Ideas for Pre-School Children
   — Two and Three Year Olds

CHURCH HOUSE PARTY

Even the smallest children can be taught to love the house of God. Love for the church will develop within children long before they can understand its deeper theological meaning if the happiest experiences they ever enjoy are centered around the church and people who love the church. This party need not be held in a fellowship room or Sunday school room on the church property for it can be planned with equal effectiveness in a private home.

Decorations

The best single decoration for a Church House Party is a large improvised church building in the center of the room. The type building and construction will depend entirely on local resources. The "building" should be constructed in a manner which allows the children to walk in and out of it. Two game tables placed end to end and covered with cloth may form the entrance to the church. The roof may be improvised of cardboard and topped with a steeple. Display supply houses in the larger cities often have these kinds of buildings ready made, even emulating stained glass windows. To make the church house complete, a bell may be placed to ring in the steeple or soft music may be heard from a record player inside the structure. If this church is planned creatively and constructed well, a lasting impression will be made on some happy and fortunate little boys and girls.

Things to Do

(1) *Singing.* No party centered around a church house would be complete without robust singing by the boys and girls. The choruses and songs they know best will be the ones they enjoy singing most.

(2) *Story time.* Resources for telling are as big as the church itself. Flannelgraph, Bible story books, record players, and clever, dedicated Sunday school teachers may be worked together into a story time the children will love.

(3) *Marching.* If the children have been sitting long (and their attention span is probably no longer than ten minutes) it will be a good break for adults and children if the boys and girls can be led in a march around the church and through the room.

(4) *Object lesson.* A bell which actually rings may be used to tell the children about church bells which make people happy and announce to the world that services are beginning in God's house.

(5) *Rhythm band.* Pots and pans, an oatmeal box containing a few marbles, a shoe box drum, toy instruments and other things may be used to improvise a rhythm band which tiny tots will enjoy.

(6) *Quiet time.* Before refresh-

ments are served it may be well to ask all the children to lie down on the floor, or to place their heads on their folded hands for a few moments of quietness before they are served their food.

(7) *Treasure box.* Supply houses have small treasure chests filled with inexpensive trinkets for boys and girls. These toys cost only pennies apiece but can be the source of immense joy to little folks.

(8) *Meet the pastor.* If the pastor's schedule can be adjusted for him to drop in on the party for a few moments, it may help the boys and girls more fully to understand who he is and perhaps learn to know him better.

Refreshments
Chocolate milk
Individual cakes in the shape of a church or church bell
Soft mints

Devotions

If the pastor is able to visit the party it may be well to have him tell a three minute story and then lead in prayer. Not every pastor is a good storyteller for tiny children but every pastor will know how to say an appropriate prayer for boys and girls.

Another suggestion for devotions at the church house party is the story of little Samuel who was brought to the Temple by his mother where he actually lived in the church house.

NOAH'S ARK PARTY

To tiny tots, no story is more exciting than the thrilling tale about Noah and his big boat which was filled with all kinds of animals. Small children learning to play are early introduced to exciting experiences, playing with tiny boats, etc. And they love all kinds of animals. Tiny children often think of these animals in the same manner they do persons, and are shocked during their early maturation process to learn that animals do not actually speak. A little planning around the animal-boat theme for this party will make a great and lasting impression on these tiny folks. It is easy to make this a Bible-centered party experience.

Decorations

Without fail, the party should center around some kind of a sizable boat which is built in the room where the party is being held. This could be a large boat painted on paper against the wall. It could be a ship improvised basically from a rowboat brought in for the occasion, but, whatever your resources and imagination will provide, be sure to have a boat which can dramatize the meaning of Noah's Ark to these small people.

Also, there are many department stores and toy shops which now have large stuffed animals as big as human beings: giraffes and elephants are particularly popular among the toy makers. It may be worthwhile to contact these people to see if large animals might be borrowed as decorations for the Noah's Ark party.

Things to Do

(1) *Name the animals.* Tiny tots enjoy the challenge of identifying both domestic and wild animals. Pictures of these animals are available in nearly all children's books. Actual toy animals may be available in some places. A small animal cookie or candy may be given to each child as he identifies the animal on display.

(2) *The story of Noah's Ark.* Several professional groups have produced the story of Noah's Ark for children on records, complete with music and sound effects. Also, the story is graphically told in many children's Bible story books. Do not pass by the possibility of the impact being made by the teacher who can tell well the story of God who directed his friend Noah to build a huge boat which would hold all the animals.

(3) *Animal hunt.* If the children attending this party are fairly well-developed as three-year-olds, they may enjoy the challenge of hunting the little toy animals hidden about the room. Packages of these inexpensive animals may be purchased. Allow the children to keep the animals which they find. It may be well to have an extra supply of animals for any less mature child who is not able to keep up with the rest in the hunt.

Obviously the animals should not be hidden too well.

(4) *Free time.* Tiny tots always know how to make the most of time which is not scheduled. They are not cooperative and tend to amuse themselves in a variety of ways. Their built-in resistance to regimentation will help them make the most of unscheduled time.

(5) *Rocking horse ride.* One or even several rocking horses can be used for a most happy time with these small tots. Turns must be planned if there are not enough rocking horses for each of them.

(6) *Color animals.* Numerous coloring books with pictures of animals are available for small children. A low table or space on the floor may be provided for this entertainment. Since tiny children tend to want the colors others have, it may be well to have a good supply of only a few of the most used colors.

Refreshments

A box of animal crackers for every child is sure to make a big hit. These may be eaten either at the party or given as departing gifts to the children. Also, candy in the shape of boats is often available. Most bakery shops can provide decorated cakes in the shape of a boat.

Devotions

The Bible contains a beautiful little story about a dove Noah released from the ark. It quickly returned the first time because it could not find a place to light; the second time it brought a twig of a tree; and the third time it never returned. The storyteller may hold a bird figure or picture in her hand while telling the story. The lesson may be suggested that God loves all the animals.

BALLOON PARTY

No single play object is loved more universally by children than the balloon. A balloon is colorful, light, easy to hold, and it bounces all around. It is decorative, inexpensive, and may be supplied in great numbers. No little tiny child will ever feel a party that features balloons is a failure.

Decorations

A number of balloons may be suspended from the ceiling. A baby's crib may be filled heaping-high with inflated balloons. Balloons of any color, shape and size may be used.

Things to Do

(1) *Tell the colors.* Challenge the children to identify the colors of several balloons as they are held up in succession. Give the balloon to the child as he identifies the color.

(2) *Make balloon animals.* In many areas there are men who specialize in making balloons into animal figures, or balloons may be bought at stores selling sleight-of-hand supplies. With a little practice you will learn how to keep children spellbound making animals from balloons.

(3) *Send up the Gospel.* Write gospel messages or Sunday school invitations on pieces of paper which are enclosed or attached to balloons inflated with helium gas. Gather the children for a brief prayer and then release a great number of these balloons into the air. The children will be delighted beyond words to see balloons rise into the air and disappear.

(4) *Story time.* An imaginative person may well invent a happy missionary story about the balloon that got lost and sailed across the ocean to a foreign land. To hold the attention of these small children, the story must be short and simple.

(5) *Make bubbles.* Besides watching the balloons move about, children enjoy seeing bubbles created. They will be fascinated to watch them sail through the air to explode against a wall or some other object. The teacher or leader of the party may blow the bubbles for the children and give opportunity for a few of the older ones to try this skill by themselves.

(6) *Free time.* If a room can be filled with balloons and the children given free opportunity to play, they will amuse themselves no end with kicking, running, squealing, and otherwise enjoying the experience of playing with balloons.

Refreshments

Clown ice cream. Place a dipper of vanilla ice cream on a dessert plate. On the "face" place an inverted cone to form the clown hat. Make three pom-poms on the hat with dabs of whipped cream. Features of the face may be made of chocolate or butterscotch chips, pieces of maraschino cherries, miniature marshmallows, and cinnamon candies. Every clown face may be different. Serve immediately before the clowns melt.

Devotions

Many little children this age are able to say their own prayers. If encouraged, several of the children may join in a series of prayers which will serve as devotions for the party. Besides asking the children to speak to God, it may be well after a period of quietness to ask them what God has said to them. Their answers not only may be devotional but disarming.

A RAINBOW PARTY

The Bible story of the rainbow which appeared in the sky at the end of the flood may be used as the theme for a very happy hour for the tiny tots you want to entertain and teach. This party may be used as a follow-up on the Noah's Ark party. Most of the small children will have heard and been impressed by the story of how the rainbow came to be. The imaginative use of bright colors will be helpful in impressing this theme on the children.

Decorations

Ordinary strips of colored crepe paper may be purchased in the stationery store for the construction of a huge rainbow which can go the full length and height of a wall in the room where the party is to be held. The size of the rainbow will depend somewhat on the available space. If a mirror or large window is available, the rainbow may be painted directly on its surface. A poster paint can be used which dissolves easily. Also, glass wax with food coloring may be used as a window paint. The rainbow may be seen by the children from outside as well as inside.

Things to Do

(1) *Name the colors of the rainbow.* Children this age can be challenged by trying to name their colors. The older ones will probably know most of the primary colors.

(2) *Rainbow name tags.* Each child may be given a beautiful tag which has on it the colors of the rainbow. Print the name of the child with a felt pen. This may be attached with a safety pin and will serve as a souvenir of the party.

(3) *Records.* Many songs about rainbows and even the story of the first rainbow are available on records from Christian supply centers. Besides listening to the records, the children may be taught some of the songs. They will enjoy singing along with the record.

(4) *Paint rainbows.* If the space and materials are available, children this age enjoy painting. They can do either finger painting or brush painting with water colors. Old white shirts or other protective garments may be used to keep them from spoiling party clothes. Color books often have rainbows in them for children to paint.

(5) *Rainbow prizes.* Multi-colored sacks of trinkets may be given to the boys and girls to play with at the party or at departure time to take home. A visit to the variety store may prove helpful in this regard.

(6) *Informal play.* Never underestimate the joy of small children at informal play. They love to talk to each other, giggle, and copy each other's actions. Although the play

may be informal, this does not mean it should be unsupervised.

Refreshments

Rainbow ice cream or sherbet will help fit the theme of this party. If these are not available, perhaps Neapolitan ice cream is.

Triangle jelly sandwiches with tinted bread may be tasty and particularly appealing to the tiny ones. Also, small children often love diced fruit in whipped cream, particularly if it is colored pink. Milk may be served for the drink.

Devotions

Use the rainbow theme to teach the children the meaning of a "promise." Ask the boys and girls to make promises to God. The Bible story is in Genesis chapter eight.

CHRISTMAS PARTY

The two- and three-year-old children are having their first awareness of the meaning and joy connected with the annual Christmas celebration. They are particularly susceptible to the story of the baby Jesus because they are aware of babies in their own home or others they see at church. One of the first few words in their vocabulary probably is "baby." The bright colors in Christmas decorations plus the use of bells are a happy stimulation to these small ones.

Decorations

A lollipop tree on a low table may be an excellent decoration and center of interest for the Christmas party for two- and three-year-olds. The lollipops should eventually be given to the children. An artificial tree which is available in most Christmas decoration shops can be best used for the lollipop tree.

Also, Christmas bells make a wonderful decorating theme for two- and three-year-olds. In fact, bells may be substituted on the lollipop tree. Sleigh bells may be made for each child by using shoestrings attached to the tiny chrome bells available in Christmas decoration centers.

Things to Do

(1) *Bells on shoes.* Tie a very tiny Christmas bell on each of the children's shoes. Some may resent this and resist the bells while others will enjoy the tinkle that comes each time they move their feet about.

(2) *Bell name tags.* A fair-sized Christmas bell may be used as a name tag for each child. Actually these can make a noise or be made from cardboard.

(3) *Christmas records.* Every year brings a new deluge of beautiful Christmas music for boys and girls. These records may be used most effectively if the children are given a chance to sing with the records. Also, many of the children's records contain stories with musical backgrounds and sound effects.

(4) *Little gifts.* Sometime during the tiny tots party each child should be given a little gift which has a small bell attached to the ribbon. These gifts should be identical, helping the children feel all are treated alike. The ribbon with the bell attached may be tied around their wrist as a souvenir to take home.

(5) *Show and tell.* The older children may enjoy a "show and tell" time when they can talk about clothes they are wearing, things they see, or whatever impresses them at the moment. If caught in the right mood, these children can be very expressive.

(6) *Christmas stockings.* Few things are cuter for tiny tots than small Christmas stockings. These may be made or purchased and will be a continuing source of joy for many

of the children throughout the Christmas season. These are especially good for youngsters who may come from an underprivileged home.

(7) *A Christmas story*. The poem, "'Twas the Night Before Christmas," is available in several children's versions. Youngsters love the rhythm and feel the mood of this poem which does communicate something of the holiday spirit.

Refreshments

Marshmallow Christmas trees may be made for each child. Marshmallows often come in varied sizes and colors. An adaptation of the marshmallow Christmas tree is the marshmallow snow man which also fits the Christmas theme in some parts of the country. Pink whipped jello and cupcakes are loved by two- and three-year olds.

Devotions

Without fail the Christmas manger scene should be used for a closing devotion period. These are available in all sizes and prices. Tell, with great animation, how Jesus came to be born in the stable at Bethlehem. Be sure to indicate the presence of the animals (sheep and donkey), the shepherds, manger, and a beautiful sky filled with stars. The figure of an angel may be suspended above the manger or held in the hand of the storyteller to indicate the Christmas message of good will.

BIRTHDAY PARTY

Second, third and fourth birthdays of pre-schoolers are big occasions. Most psychologists indicate the child should have no more guests present than he has candles on his cake. However, for small children growing up in Sunday school classes, it is often good for the child to feel that he, particularly, is being featured, along with the children with whom he associates week by week. Since birthday celebrations often are times of unusual excitement for little tots, it is well not to have the party last more than one hour. It is not uncommon for these little folks to become physically ill through the excitement of too big a party on their second, third, or fourth birthday.

Decorations

The best decoration in the world for a birthday party is a large cake in the center of the table covered with a frosting picture, the words "Happy Birthday," and the name of the child. If the cake is large, candles up to three or four inches high may be more attractive to the children. The room may be decorated with a fairly large sign which says, "Bobby is 3." Also, children love crepe paper streamers. Several of these strung across the room may seem mighty pretty to a three-year-old.

Things to Do

(1) *Open presents*. The bringing of presents to these little children is perhaps the biggest event at the party. With little folks like these it is important for the hostess to have presents for every child, not just the one whose birthday is being observed.

(2) *Games*. If this is a fourth birthday, the children may be mature enough to enjoy a few of the simple little games, such as, "London Bridge Is Falling Down," or "Ring Around the Rosie."

(3) *Birthday records*. Record companies have produced birthday records and songs for each birthday anniversary year. For instance, there is a song for the third birthday, another for the fourth, etc.

(4) *Bible story*. Children this age may be greatly impressed with the fact that Jesus also was once a little child. Large pictures of Jesus in the years of His childhood are not difficult to acquire. One of these may be the basis for a story about Him. Emphasis may be made on the fact that Joseph was a carpenter, that Jesus probably played with the shavings which fell from the carpenter bench. It may be suggested that the area near where He lived was a fruit-growing section and Jesus may well have enjoyed playing under the trees as a small boy. These children may appreciate the fact that He traveled with Mary and Joseph on the back of a donkey.

(5) *Follow the leader*. Children of this age may be taken on an en-

joyable walk by providing them a suitable clothesline rope on which each child places his hand. Knots in the rope at intervals may indicate the place where each child is to hold. Nursery-school people are very effective in this type of activity.

Refreshments

>Peanut butter sandwiches
>Banana circles
>Vanilla pudding
>Maraschino cherry garnish
>Milk

Devotions

Since children this age are intrigued by babies and have a feeling of superiority over them, they may well enjoy the story of the famous baby Moses who was saved from the bulrushes in the Nile River. The story may be read from one of the better Bible story books or told by the teacher or hostess. Records are also available which tell the story of baby Moses.

TEDDY BEAR PARTY

The teddy bear is standard equipment for small children. Since some may have an adaptation it may be well to ask each child to bring his favorite doll, indicating to the parents that you mean stuffed toy. Teddy bears, Raggedy Anns, stuffed animals and other such things may be brought by the children.

Decorations

Perhaps the best decoration for the teddy bear party is one or more of the most huge stuffed bears or similar toys you can find. Sometimes high school girls have a supply of these. It probably would appear to be amusing to these small children if each of these huge stuffed toys was in a separate baby's crib. One might even be placed in a bassinet, set in a rocker, or otherwise placed as though it were a live child.

Things to Do

(1) *Conversation time.* Besides providing seats for each child, provide an adjoining seat for the teddy bear or other toy the child brings. Give the children opportunity for free time conversation with their animals and each other.

(2) *Story time.* All little children this age enjoy the thrilling excitement in the classic story of "Goldilocks and the Three Bears." A little drama, gestures, and change of voices will help to make the story more exciting.

(3) *"Smokey the Bear."* One of the most famous and popular current figures in wooded and mountainous sections of America is "Smokey the Bear." Check local resources for figures, cardboard cutouts and other things concerning "Smokey the Bear" that might well be adapted to your party.

(4) *Introductions.* Ask each child to introduce his own "teddy" by name and tell anything about it he may desire.

(5) *Name tags.* A felt pen may be used to write on inch-wide ribbon the name of each child and the name of his teddy bear. Pin these on both the children and on the toys.

(6) *Rocking chair.* Turns may be taken in a rocking chair for each child to rock his own doll or animal to sleep. This rocking chair may prove to be the most popular piece of furniture in the house.

Refreshments

Teddy Bear cookies*
Cocoa and marshmallows
Kool-aid or fruit juice

Devotions

The Bible indicates David once slew a bear. A teacher or hostess with some imagination may be able to tell a story around this incident. Also, children may be asked to indicate a time when they feel God helped them to do something special. They may feel He helped them to open a door, go to sleep, find a lost toy, or whatever! Close with prayers of thankfulness for His help.

* See Party Recipes section in back of book.

BIBLE STORY HOUR

A Bible story hour may not be the most original idea but it can be a most appreciated experience by small children. They love to hear stories and fortunately the Bible is full of them. All sorts of aids are now available to make Bible stories more interesting. Visual aids range from simple to complex. The development of the story hour depends largely on your own resources and desires.

Decorations

Many Sunday school publishing companies produce large pictures which relate directly to Sunday school stories. Some of these may be put together to form a large book which you may use as decorations for the children, indicating the fact that God's Word is filled with stories of His love for children. If the making of a book is not practical, then the story pictures may be displayed on easels or attached to the wall.

Things to Do

(1) *Visual aids.* Flannelback pictures which can be attached easily to a flannel-covered background are available in many forms for the graphic telling of Bible stories. Some publishing companies are now producing large-sized Bible figures to illustrate the stories teachers tell. Certainly these are helpful in providing the children with a better presentation of God's Word.

(2) *Big pictures.* Several murals are available from Sunday school supply companies which may be used for the telling of a marvelous story. These murals generally run four feet high and eight to twelve feet long. They can also be secured in a three-by-five-foot size. The mural may be used for several Bible story hours as the story is continued about the particular background indicated in the mural.

(3) *Records.* There is no end to the number of excellent Bible story records now available.

(4) *Stories with sound effects.* Children may be taught to enjoy stories in which they actually provide the sound effects themselves. When the name of a certain person is mentioned they make one type of noise and when another place or thing is mentioned they respond with a given sound. The children may have some difficulty in adapting to this unless they are fairly mature little folks.

(5) *Songs.* Every Sunday school teacher has a resource of songs based on Bible stories. Children love to sing these and will love them all the more if there are pictures available which relate to the songs, or if they can relate the song to a story which has just been told.

(6) *Figures.* The large figures which

are now available from Sunday school publishing houses to illustrate Bible stories may be best appreciated if these little folks can hold them in their hands. A twelve-inch high figure of David held in the hands of a little boy is much more meaningful than one held by the teacher at a distance.

Refreshments

Cookies and chocolate milk may be enough refreshments for the children who have enjoyed a wonderful story hour together. This may be particularly true if the Bible story hour is to be repeated fairly often. Heavy refreshments often do not fit well into the schedules of small children.

Devotions

Ask three of the older children to come forward and pray prayers of their own making. There may be prayer requests which the other children suggest. Even at this early age children can be taught to have concern in prayer.

VALENTINE PARTY

With the exception of Christmas there probably is no holiday in the year that tiny tots like better than Valentine's Day. The bright colors, picture cards, ribbons and other paraphernalia used to observe Valentine's Day are especially attractive to little folks.

Decorations

Heart-shaped valentines on the walls attached to the draperies and curtains, and on the windows, can be exciting for these young children. In addition, the table may be decorated with a bright red and white valentine cake. It may be inscribed, "I love you."

Things to Do

(1) *Heart hunt.* Suitably wrapped candies of heart shape may be hidden around the room for the children to find and either eat on the spot or store in their pockets for later use.

(2) *Who do you love?* The children may be asked to tell who it is they love best. Although their tendency may be to keep their "love" within the immediate family, they may be encouraged to include the teacher and other children in their list.

(3) *Story time.* The story of Moses' mother and how she loved her baby will be intriguing to these children.

(4) *Scripture verse.* "God is love" is an excellent verse to teach the children at this party.

(5) *Valentines.* Some valentines are suitable for little children to enjoy. Some may be purchased which can be colored with crayons by the children. The children may be directed in making a valentine from construction paper to present to their mothers.

Refreshments

Sandwiches made with pink bread
Valentine cake
Strawberry ice cream
Milk

Devotions

Ask each of the children to say a prayer for those they love most. Or have the children repeat each phrase of a prayer which is given to them by the teacher or hostess.

COWBOY PARTY

Even the smallest children soon learn to play the part of the American cowboy. The children will look cute in cowboy boots and hats. A few extra cowboy straw hats may be available for those children who do not have any special cowboy clothes of their own to wear to the party.

Decorations

The amount and type of decorations for this party will depend on whether it is scheduled for outdoors or inside, in a recreation room or the living room of a home, and on the general resources of cowboy paraphernalia available. Bales of straw, real or play saddles, rocking horses, a corral fence, a tent or lean-to, and Western blankets may be part of the materials which can be used for decorations.

Things to Do

(1) *Singing*. A guitar or an accordian are excellent instruments for the accompaniment to the singing of the children. The instruments themselves probably will be great entertainment for the boys and girls.

(2) *Horses*. In one way or another, horses should be worked into the entertainment for the children. They may color with crayons, look at pictures, or ride stick horses.

(3) *Show and tell*. Give each child an opportunity to show his cowboy clothes and tell about his cowboy gear.

(4) *Story time*. Children's story books are filled with episodes which follow the cowboy theme. A clever teacher or hostess, however, may be able to use the Bible story of Abraham and his nephew Lot, whose herdsmen quarreled making it necessary to divide their land. This is a real live cowboy theme right from the book of Genesis.

Refreshments

Sugared Doughnuts
Individual boxes of raisins
Cold milk

Devotions

Tell the children how Jesus loved boys and girls while He was here on earth. A picture may be available which shows Jesus surrounded by the children. A story may be improvised on this theme.

PICNIC

Almost everyone loves a picnic. Little children hear their older brothers and sisters and parents talk about the picnics they enjoy. All that is needed for a picnic with little folks is sunshine and a grassy plot of ground, public or private. While most parties for two- and three-year-olds are no longer than one hour, a picnic may last twice this long because of the informality and the open spaces.

Decorations

There are no decorations for a picnic. A suitable spot must be found, perhaps a city park with a pond where the ducks swim. A grassy, shady spot may be located where blankets may be placed on the ground for the children to rest and enjoy their lunch. They just might like to take a nap.

Things to Do

(1) *Feeding time.* If the picnic can be scheduled for an area where ducks, pigeons, seagulls, or squirrels gather, the children will be intensely interested in feeding and watching the birds or animals.

(2) *Hike.* A walk through the park, especially along the paths where flowers can be seen readily by little children is excellent. They will investigate many things along the way, including flowers, water fountains, park furniture and anything else they can see and touch.

(3) *Flowers.* As a gift to take home, each child may be presented with a flower. It may be well that these are artificial flowers made of bright colors. They may be attached to a buttonhole or pinned on the child's clothing.

Refreshments

A picnic basket might contain sandwiches, cookies, bananas and apples. It is best not to use fork and spoon foods with the little ones. A thermos of Kool-aid will be a treat. Also investigate the possibility of buying ice cream cones at the park "stand."

Devotions

With the children seated on the blankets, the hostess may direct them in singing some choruses and then tell the story of Jesus feeding the five thousand people with the lunch provided by a little boy.

OTHER LANDS PARTY

A small child thinks everyone is like the people in his own family. However, as children begin to move out into the world through Sunday school they become aware that other people may be different. Although little can be done to teach children this age the meaning of missions, they may enjoy a party around the theme of children in other lands.

Decorations
Big beautiful travel folders on Holland, Africa, India, the Orient, and South America may be chosen for the party decorations.

Things to Do
(1) *Doll display.* Dolls representing other nations may be shown to the children. However, none should be shown which the children cannot touch. They are interested primarily in things they can feel.

(2) *Choruses.* Most little children have been taught a number of missionary choruses in Sunday school such as "Jesus Loves the Little Children of the World" and "For God So Loved the World."

(3) *Boats and planes.* The children may be interested in looking at, feeling, and talking about small boats and planes which represent the transportation from our country to another. Ships, outrigger canoes, sailboats and other means of transportation may be demonstrated with small replicas.

(4) *Other races.* A good object lesson and first step toward keeping prejudice from ever beginning with small children is to let them play with youngsters of other races.

(5) *Sand box.* Free time play in a large sand box is loved by children of this age. Small boats, planes and other toys which represent travel may be used by the children in the sand box.

Refreshments
A cake decorated with small flags of foreign countries may be cut with the children watching. Serve with fruit punch.

Devotions
If children of other races have been invited to the party, and especially if they are a little older, they may bring devotions by leading in several short prayers.

PLAYGROUND PARTY

Any public or private playground which may be scheduled exclusively for an hour's use by two- and three-year-olds, is an excellent setting for a party for them. Churches, nursery schools, public parks, recreation centers, and even some restaurants have special play areas for children. These should be reserved exclusively for the tiny tots to make this party a success.

Decorations

No decorations are needed for this party. The playground equipment itself is sufficient. However, if the hostess feels the need, she may attach balloons and streamers to the equipment already available. A huge sand box, a series of swings, a jungle gym, and a slide are all exciting to the little children. Some playgrounds have odd-shaped structures and interesting combinations of concrete pipes over and through which the children may play. Supervision is all important.

Things to Do

(1) *Free time*. All of the play at this party is informal and constantly supervised. Especially when children are playing on new toys and in new circumstances they are susceptible to feelings of anxiety and even accident. They often fail to know their limits.

(2) *Raisins*. Each child may be given his own tiny box of raisins. From time to time each child will interrupt his play to enjoy another little treat from the box.

(3) *Blanket*. One or more blankets will be needed where the children can come to rest and get the reassurance they need from the presence of an adult. Children this age often abruptly break their play and without seeming provocation run to the feet of an adult nearby. This needed reassurance soon sends them back to enjoy their play again. The blanket may also be used as a refreshment center or even a place for a nap.

(4) *Balls*. Some children will enjoy the added play provided by the presence of a large utility ball. It may be rolled, kicked, thrown, or just watched.

(5) *Song games*. Older children may enjoy joining together for such song games as "Here We Go 'round the Mulberry Bush," or "The Farmer in the Dell."

(6) *Candy hunt*. The children may enjoy hunting for candy which the leader has spread around the area.

(7) *Follow the leader*. The older children may enjoy a game of follow the leader. This may take them over, around, through, and on various play equipment.

Refreshments

    Peanut butter sandwiches
    Bottled orange drink

Devotions

After a vigorous play experience the children may be brought together on the blanket for a story time. The teacher may be able to give a highly intriguing, interesting, imaginative account of the visit Jesus made to the temple when He was a little boy. The entire play session may be closed with a prayer by the leader.

II. Party Ideas for Kindergarten Children — Four and Five Year Olds

SNOW PARTY

In many parts of the country boys and girls have the opportunity to enjoy snow during winter months. When the earliest snows have fallen and the beauty of winter is at its best, the small boys and girls will enjoy a snow party.

Decorations

No special decorations are needed for a snow party. God has provided these decorations with His own handiwork which covers the trees and the ground. However, a cotton snow man in the center of the table may make a lovely centerpiece for the children at refreshment time.

Things to Do

(1) *Snow ice cream.* A lovely ice cream dish for children may be made with the combination of clean snow, milk or cream, sugar, and a dash of vanilla flavoring. This may be served with bright plastic spoons.

(2) *Sleigh ride.* The kind of ride to be given the children in the snow will depend on local resources. A horse drawn sleigh, toboggans, or steel-runner sleds may be used. In all events there must be good adult supervision to avoid accident. In some instances the children may enjoy a hayride through the snow even though the wagon is on wheels instead of runners.

(3) *Snow man.* If conditions are right the boys and girls will be intrigued with the opportunity to contribute toward making a big snow man. Size and elaborateness of construction will depend on the condition of the snow and the planning of the adults in charge.

(4) *New paths.* If the snow is fresh the boys and girls may enjoy making new paths in areas where no one has yet walked.

Refreshments

Softened Philadelphia cream cheese on assorted crackers
Hot steaming cocoa with marshmallows
Snow white vanilla frosted cupcakes

Devotions

During the devotional period the adult in charge may tell the children how God has made each of the four seasons in the year for its own purpose and our happiness. Much may be said about the beauty of winter while the earth sleeps. The children may be asked to say prayers of thankfulness to God for the beautiful earth.

MAY BASKET PARTY

There is an old-fashioned custom in some parts of the United States where people on the first day of May take baskets of flowers anonymously to the homes of their friends. Since this idea adapts itself to the kindergarten boys and girls, a party may be planned around this time.

Decorations

Either outdoors or in a room, a baby's play pen may be filled with artificial grass and huge artificial flowers. A large handle may be constructed in an arch over the top of the play pen to create the idea of a basket.

Things to Do

The entire time of the party may be spent in the construction and decoration of the May baskets to be delivered to parents or relatives. Selections of construction materials, coloring supplies, artificial grass, flowers, and appropriate materials for making cards should be in ample supply. The adults in charge should direct the children in undertaking no more than they could finish in a fairly short period of time. After the baskets have been completed, they may be delivered to the various homes before the children return to the original party place for refreshments and closing devotions.

Refreshments

Delicious May baskets *
Cold milk
Pastel mint wafers

Devotions

The story of the "Strange Visitors at Abraham's Tent-home" is recorded in the eighteenth chapter of Genesis. This story may be used to help teach the children about the joy of visitors to our homes and the joy of visiting in the homes of others.

---

* See Party Recipes section in back of book.

MISSIONARY PARTY

The idea of missions is not fully understood by kindergarten children. They are conscious though of children in other lands who look different and dress different than themselves. Four- and five-year-olds are also aware that many of these children are hungry and less fortunate than themselves. However, children in church schools are aware of missionaries and the feeling of responsibility the church has for people in other parts of the world. Four- and five-year-old children today know a great deal more about the entire world than their counterparts a generation ago.

Decorations

Large travel posters which are available from airline companies and travel agencies are colorful and certainly impressive decorations for the kindergarten children. Also, within the resources of many churches are missionary curios which are captivating to children.

Things to Do

(1) *Hats.* If the local resources are equal to the challenge, the boys and girls will find a good deal of enjoyment in wearing native hats representing foreign lands. These might include Chinese coolie hats, sombreros from south of the border, flower leis from the South Pacific, fur caps from the northlands, and turbans from India.

(2) *Native beads.* Many people to whom missionaries minister are fond of bright decorations made of colored beads. The boys and girls may make their own native beads with the use of string and uncooked macaroni which may be colored, or with the use of small wooden blocks with holes for stringing.

(3) *Costumes.* Many children have costumes available representing foreign cultures. The children will enjoy attending the party dressed in these.

(4) *Missionary story.* A resourceful individual may tell an imaginary missionary story using the curio objects available through the resources of the church. Snake skins, hatchets, art objects, and other mementos may be used to dramatically illustrate the story of a child in a foreign land.

(5) *Missionary songs.* In many communities there are persons who can teach the children a familiar Sunday school chorus in a foreign language, such as Spanish or French. Kindergarten children can learn a foreign language song almost as quickly as they can learn one in English.

(6) *Filmstrips.* Most denominational publishing houses and many independent organizations have excellent supplies of missionary filmstrips. Often the filmstrips are ac-

companied by records which amplify the film.

Refreshments

Meat loaf
Mashed potatoes   Green peas
Carrot strips
Chocolate pudding
Milk

Devotions

The story of Philip, the first missionary to an Ethiopian, is recorded in Acts 8:26-40. Following the reading or telling of this story, the children may be asked to lead in prayers for boys and girls in other lands.

BUNNY HUNT

Although many Christians wish there were a way to keep Easter free from colored eggs, little yellow ducks, and bunnies, it is a fact that children and adults alike in the United States have the coming of Spring, new fashions, and fairy tales about Easter bunnies all confused with the occasion the church has for celebrating the resurrection of our Lord. However, the hunting for Easter eggs and the anticipation for colorful baskets of candy and eggs on Easter morning does not seem to have affected the piety of most children from Christian families. Easter is a season for happiness among children and is considered by many the occasion for an Easter party celebration. Perhaps it is better for the teacher or hostess to keep the idea of the resurrection of Christ completely separate from the other functions of the party until time for closing devotions. As the story of the resurrection of Jesus is told during the devotional time the explanation may be made of the real meaning of Easter.

Decorations

A large table outside may be used as the center for the Easter decorations. The table should be covered with a cloth which comes almost to the floor. Pin huge colored paper eggs on the hanging of the tablecloth. A stuffed bunny in a nest of artificial paper grass or green nylon net may occupy the center of the table. Invitations may be written with felt pens on hard boiled eggs which are decorated with flower seals.

Things to Do

(1) *Easter egg hunt.* If there is a wide range in age and competence among the children, it will be best to divide them into age groups and assign each a separate place for hunting the Easter eggs.

(2) *Bunny hunt.* Along with the Easter eggs, marshmallow bunnies wrapped in foil may be hidden. When found these may be redeemed for special prizes.

(3) *Pictures.* Use a Polaroid camera to take pictures of the children while they are deeply involved in the concentration of the hunt. These may be given to the children as souvenirs of the day.

(4) *Cards.* Bright Easter cards may be given each child as a special favor. The cards may be used as place cards at refreshment time.

(5) *Coloring books.* Either a page or an entire coloring book on Easter bunnies may be given to the children as a part of their free time entertainment.

(6) *Bunny hop.* At refreshment time ask each of the children to hop on one foot from a given point to their place at the table.

(7) *Live bunny.* Nearly all four- and five-year-olds will enjoy the experience of touching a live bunny if one can be at hand.

Refreshments

Serve egg-shaped sandwiches with various fillings, accompanied by celery and carrot strips.

Decorate Easter egg cupcakes by frosting and then covering with multi-color coconut; while frosting is still moist place several jelly beans on the nest.

Serve ice cold lemonade as the beverage.

Devotions

The story of the resurrection of Christ from the tomb is told by each of the four gospel writers. The passages are Matthew 28:2-20, Mark 16:5-14; Luke 24:4-12; and John 20:2-18. This beautiful story may be read to the children from the King James Version, from one of the standard Bible story books, or may be told extemporaneously. A point will no doubt be made of the real meaning of Easter. If possible, a closing prayer may be given by the pastor, Sunday school superintendent, or other church leader.

OUTDOOR PARTY

At the right season of the year, especially in the late spring, boys and girls enjoy a party outdoors. Since these are four- and five-year-old children the best place will be a large fenced yard, or a properly supervised public park area. In some cities, park areas may be reserved for small children. If possible there should be a large sandbox, ample play area on the grass, and possibly children's attractions such as slides, swings and teeter-totters.

Decorations

The only decorations needed for an outdoor party are a central table and benches, or blanket spread on the ground, which the children know is occupied by the adult in charge. Children this age may sometimes feel panicky in strange circumstances and need the reassurance which comes from going to the "home" spot where the adult in charge is situated. There should be drinking water, cookies and facilities for cleansing dirty hands and faces.

Things to Do

(1) *Follow the leader.* An older child may be the leader of the group to take a march over, around, through, and across whatever obstacles may be at hand. This may sometimes be done to the accompaniment of their own singing.

(2) *Hide and seek.* By this age children are ready to be introduced to a simple version of hide and seek. The teacher may explain the rules and be *It* for the first round of the game.

(3) *Bubble blowing.* Inexpensive equipment may be secured to give the children an opportunity to blow enormous numbers of bubbles. They will find great joy in watching them emerge, drift away, and finally explode.

(4) *Free time.* A great amount of free time should be provided the boys and girls to play as they desire in the sandbox and on the play equipment at hand. Sand pails and shovels should be made available.

Refreshments

> Ham salad sandwiches
> Celery sticks
> Kool-aid
> Brownies

Devotions

Just prior to refreshments the children may be seated for story time. The Bible is filled with stories to captivate the attention of boys and girls. Among them is the story of a boy's lunch basket and a great miracle. It is recorded in Matthew 14:12-23; Mark 6:31-46; Luke 9:10-17; and John 6:1-15. Following the reading or telling of this story the boys and girls may give prayers of thanks for the picnic lunch to be served.

JONAH AND THE WHALE

One of the exciting stories for boys and girls is the tale about the Prophet Jonah and the big fish. It captures the imagination of boys and girls and therefore may be the theme for an exciting and even instructive party.

Decorations

Fish should be the theme for decorations. At an Oriental store, large decorative paper fish may be purchased which can be hung from the ceiling in a party room. Other people may make their own large fish. A gold fish bowl can prove popular as a center of interest — as long as it is kept out of reach of little hands!

Things to Do

(1) *Fishing pond.* Let every child hold a fish pole in turn and put it over a sight barrier such as a hanging curtain, upright piano, or divan where an older individual secures a little gift to the fishing line. These gifts become prizes for each person.

(2) *The mouth of the fish.* If the mouth of a large fish can be painted and constructed on heavy duty pressed board or plywood, the boys and girls will find great entertainment in attempting to roll a ball through the mouth of the fish.

(3) *Free time.* A card table covered completely with a blanket may be one of the improvised toys for the boys and girls for their free time play period. They may imagine the dark area under the table to be the inside of the great fish.

(4) *Story drama.* The boys and girls may enjoy acting out the parts of this story. Assign a child to each part including Jonah, the whale, God, the storm, and Nineveh.

(5) *Modeling clay.* The boys and girls may enjoy an opportunity to model small fish from clay which they may form easily with their fingers.

Refreshments

Tuna fish salad
on lettuce bed
Pickles   Olives
Toast triangles
Orangeade

Devotions

My Picture Story Bible by Dena Korfker* has an excellent account on the prophet who tried to run away from God. The Bible record is given in chapters one through four of Jonah. The children should be taught through this story that men love and obey God rather than fear and run from Him.

---

* Zondervan.

JACK-O'-LANTERN PARTY

Hallowe'en is the time when sweet little goblins enjoy dressing up to frighten adults and to play imaginary games about imaginary witches, gobblins, and "real-live" speaking pumpkins. Kindergarten folks enjoy Hallowe'en parties but the sponsors must remember that four- and five-year-olds scare easily. They are happy to assume frightening roles themselves but respond negatively when others do so. Therefore, the theme of Hallowe'en should be followed but the scary elements of the occasion must be eliminated from the kindergarten party.

Decorations

The boys and girls will enter the party room through a tunnel of orange and black crepe streamers and orange balloons hanging from the ceiling of the hall way. The party room centers around a table decorated with an orange covering striped in black. A jack-o'-lantern centerpiece can be very attractive. In many communities, hanging jack-o'-lanterns which are lighted from the inside may be purchased for further party decoration.

Things to Do

(1) *Spider game*. Each child is given an individual black string which takes him back and forth to all parts of the room where he finally arrives at a prize tied to the opposite end of the string.

(2) *Candle light*. The boys and girls may enjoy a contest of blowing out the candle. Or without the element of competition they may simply enjoy the experience of blowing out the light.

(3) *Mystery tunnel*. An exciting mystery tunnel may be constructed of game tables or chairs aligned with each other and covered over with brown wrapping paper.

(4) *Popcorn*. Kindergarten people are intrigued by watching kernels of corn pop into beautiful white flakes which taste so very good. Pop the corn in a kettle, letting some of the popped kernels fall on the floor which is covered with paper and children.

(5) *Witches race*. The children may be divided into two groups. Each group is given a tall black hat and a witch's broom. The children take turns riding the witch's broom with the great tall black hat on their heads. They may either compete in a relay race or simply enjoy riding with the broom and the hat.

(6) *Apple float*. Since these children are not able to bob for apples, they may enjoy choosing one of many apples which are floating in a container of water.

(7) *Paper masks*. Although the children may be frightened at each other if regular Hallowe'en masks are worn, they have considerable fun from

making their own masks out of brown paper sacks.

Refreshments

> Powdered sugar doughnuts
> Cocoa with marshmallows
> Candy corn kernels

Devotions

An interesting story for kindergarten children is the account of "the little boy whose mother lent him to the Lord." This record is given in I Samuel 1:1-3, 18.

GINGERBREAD BOY PARTY

Since little folks in kindergarten love to be about the kitchen enjoying the smells and activity of food in preparation, a teacher or hostess may entertain a small group of children with great success at a gingerbread boy party. A huge kitchen-family room arrangement is probably the best setting for this type of party.

Decorations

The best decoration for this type of party is no decoration at all, but the mouth-watering odor of fresh-baked cookies in the house. Each child should be given a place at the table where he will work in decorating and also be served refreshments. The first sheet of cookies should be scheduled to come hot from the oven giving off a wonderful aroma just as the guests arrive.

Things to Do

(1) *Puzzles.* Individual picture puzzles may be given to the children to work while the cooking continues. These puzzles should not be too difficult.

(2) *Story time.* A reader or storyteller may present the narrative of the gingerbread boy. A library copy of this tale may be secured with large illustrations to be shown the children.

(3) *Stuffed animal parade.* Each child may be given a stuffed animal to hold above his or her head while all engage in a marching time. A record player or piano can furnish the music for marching.

(4) *Decorating time.* The gingerbread cookies may be decorated by the children using raisins, chocolate chips, maraschino cherries and other things to make faces, buttons and shoes. The hostess may use a pastry tube of white frosting for added details on the cookies.

(5) *Souvenir.* Before each child leaves, give him a gingerbread man complete with his own name written in icing.

Refreshments

    Gingerbread cookies*
    Apple wedges
    Cold milk

Devotions

The story of the widow who baked a cake for Elijah is recorded in I Kings 17:8-24. The telling of this story will be appropriate at a cookie baking party for small children. The devotional period may close with prayers of thanks for the food.

---

* See Party Recipes section in back of book.

PILGRIM PARTY

November is the time boys and girls of all ages are thinking about Thanksgiving and the coming holiday season. Newspaper advertisements, television programs, and projects by older children in school all indicate Thanksgiving is in the air. Since Thanksgiving and the story of the pilgrims often are related directly to the church and Sunday school emphasis in the Fall, a Pilgrim Party may be both fun and educational.

Decorations

One of the nicest ways to decorate for a Pilgrim Party is to make a large horn-of-plenty on a low table easily visible to the boys and girls. Artificial fruit and vegetables plus real pumpkins, squash, cornstalks, and bright flowers may be used to produce a very striking effect. Under the right circumstances the plans may be made for the children to bring items which can be contributed to the horn-of-plenty. Also, plans may be made to build the horn-of-plenty from fruits and vegetables which may later be taken by the children in a gift basket to some family who would need and appreciate the expression of generosity from the children.

Things to Do

(1) *Hats, bonnets, and headdresses.* An ample supply of pilgrim hats, pilgrim bonnets, and Indian headdresses may be provided for the boys and girls to wear during the party. These may be purchased at small expense or can be made from paper. If the supply of these items is sufficient, the children may be allowed to choose between the hat, bonnet, or Indian headdress.

(2) *Picture taking.* Pictures of the boys and girls in their party headgear make memorable souvenirs for the children and their parents. If a Polaroid camera is available the effect of the picture taking is improved by the immediate development of the negative. However, many people prefer colored 35mm slides to black and white pictures. In this case be sure the background or the clothing each child has is colorful. If Polaroid pictures are made, the children can use party time to mount them on colored construction paper.

(3) *Pumpkin race.* For a few cents each, small pumpkins may be bought in ample supply for each child to enjoy. A race may be planned for the children to run from the starting point to a given goal and back again while carrying their pumpkins. Allow each child to keep his pumpkin to take home.

(4) *Candy corn relay.* Candy corn placed in a tablespoon may be used to increase the hazard of a relay race.

(5) *Free time.* Since children of this age particularly enjoy working independently, free time may be allowed for them to draw their own impressions of the first Thanksgiving.

(6) *Thanksgiving story.* The final activity before serving refreshments may be a story around the Thanksgiving theme. The story of the first Thanksgiving may be either read or told. Kindergarten Sunday school papers offer good Thanksgiving stories in abundance at this season of the year.

Refreshments

    Pumpkin chiffon tarts
    Whipped cream
    Chocolate milk

Devotions

While the children are seated in a circle, ask each one in turn to stand and tell why they are thankful. After all of the children have finished speaking, ask them to join hands with each other while the adult in charge leads in prayer.

FOURTH BIRTHDAY PARTY

Since birthdays are of enormous importance to kindergarten children, the occasion of a fourth birthday cannot be ignored. Although there may be a temptation to invite an unlimited number of children, it is most likely the guest of honor will have a happier time if the number of children is limited. Some suggest no more than four guests at a fourth birthday party; at least the number might be best limited to no more than six or eight.

Decorations

Since the birthday cake and the presents are the essentials in a fourth birthday party, it will be well to make the table the center for all decorations. A bright crepe paper covering may be used on the table with the decorated cake in the center. Party suppliers have decorations for these parties which are as elaborate and expensive as parents and teachers want to go. A bunch of bright balloons tied to the back of each chair creates an immediate festive atmosphere.

Things to Do

(1) *Crawl through chairs.* A "real fun" obstacle course may be laid out easily with the use of chairs through which the children may crawl, following the leader.

(2) *Paper hats.* Party favors, especially paper hats, are fun for four-year-olds. Allow them plenty of time to examine each other's hats, and to exchange their own for another if they desire.

(3) *Hunts.* A variety of items may be hidden around the home including such things as peanuts in shells, wrapped candies, miniature toys, and animals. Supply each child with a paper bag and give all an opportunity to join in the hunt. Each child is allowed to keep the things he finds. The hunt is followed by a free time in which the children are allowed to sit and play, or eat the items they have in their paper bags.

(4) *Listening time.* Just before the refreshments are to be served, seat the children in a circle for a quiet listening time. Kindergarten children are especially fascinated by stories told on records with sound effects. They also are very fond of listening to songs.

Refreshments

> Fruited strawberry jello
> Assorted finger sandwiches
> Birthday cake
> Lemonade

Devotions

While hands are joined in a circle, sing familiar Sunday school choruses and then close the party with several prayers by the children.

FIFTH BIRTHDAY PARTY

An important milestone celebrated by kindergarten people is the fifth birthday. Children are getting a little older by now and can enjoy a party more because of their ability to play together and their better physical coordination. At the fifth birthday party there may be considerably more cooperative activity among the children than at the fourth birthday party. Games now are beginning to be much more fun and organized.

Decorations

Although colored balloons and crepe paper streamers are difficult to improve on for decorating the room for a fifth birthday celebration, the party supply stores do have many cute, attractive themes for five-year-olds. Such themes as space ships, trains, animals, and cowboys are sold complete with centerpiece decorations, matching napkins, place cards, and tableclothes. Some clever people are able to spot these ideas and then make them with their own hands.

Things to Do

(1) *Marching song*. Five-year-olds love to march. With the help of a record player, tunes may be used to the endless delight of the children. The marches may be varied by changing leaders, asking each child to place his hand on the shoulder of the one in front of him, skipping, and marching backwards.

(2) *Follow the string*. Five-year-olds have become very proficient in the use of their fingers. Many are learning to tie their shoes. To capitalize on their new dexterity, place the name of a child on a small piece of paper which is attached to a string hanging over the back of a straight chair. After this long string has been wound around and through the chair in many different ways and directions, it finally is tied at the other end to a prize which the child may have when he has unwound the length of string from the rungs.

(3) *Singing games*. Children of this age particularly enjoy the traditional singing games such as "London Bridge Is Falling Down," "A Tisket, A Tasket, A Red and Yellow Basket," and "Ring Around the Rosie."

(4) *Drop the handkerchief*. By the fifth birthday party the children are ready to enjoy the age-old game of drop the handkerchief. The children stand in a circle facing each other. The child who is *It* skips around behind the circle eventually dropping the handkerchief behind another child. He then sprints around the circle as fast as he can to escape the child who has picked up the handkerchief and is now running after him.

If the child who is *It* can run fast enough he returns to the vacant space left empty by the child running with the handkerchief. If he is caught, the child remains *It*. If the runner fails to catch him, he becomes *It*.

(5) *Sock race.* Engage the children in a race which is complicated by each child running while he holds onto the tops of his socks.

(6) *Marble race.* Conduct a race among the children while each contestant is holding a tablespoon which contains two marbles. If the marbles are dropped, the child must go back to the starting line and try again.

Refreshments

    Miniature cupcakes
        Popsicles
      Candy favors

Devotions

Five-year-olds from a Sunday school background certainly have learned to pray. Read or tell the story contained in the thirty-seventh chapter of Genesis on "How the Boy Joseph Became a Slave." Then choose several of the children to lead in short prayers.

BIBLE STORY PARTY

Perhaps five-year-olds love a story as much or more than children of any other age. At least their joy of stories may be used as a basis for an entertaining and educational hour. The effectiveness of the party will depend considerably upon the capacity of the sponsors to adapt Bible story ideas and project them on a level children can appreciate and understand.

Decorations

The Sunday school may own the large mural which pictures Christ seated among the boy and girls. This can be used as a wonderful decoration backdrop for this party. If this particular mural is not available then any large size article or picture representing Jesus or the times in which He lived may be used both as decoration and illustration. Such items might include large floor size vases, live sheep, a Bible scroll, or pictures of Bible times.

Things to Do

(1) *Coloring books.* Several religious supply firms have produced Bible story coloring books which give endless delight to five-year-old children. Some of the more advanced children may be able to tell the story represented by their pictures.

(2) *Bible drama.* Boys and girls of this age may be taught Bible stories by acting out the parts. The story of David and Goliath, Daniel in the lions' den, Jonah and the whale, and many others may be subject to this simple dramatic process.

(3) *Records with sound effects.* Producers of Children's records have an increasing number of Bible stories with sound effects. Some of these stories are told by excellent narrators accompanied by professional musicians.

(4) *Memory verses.* During free time children may be given opportunity to decorate a sheet of paper on which is printed a memory verse. The length and complexity of the verse will depend entirely upon the development of the children. One of the simplest and most profound verses is "God is love."

(5) *Storytellers.* The resources of the local church may be used for presenting a Bible story to the children through cartoon illustrations, flannelgraph, pictures, or object lessons.

Refreshments

Miniature ice cream cones topped with an animal cracker

Devotions

Since the entire party has centered around Bible stories, an appropriate closing devotion may consist of a Sunday school chorus and prayer, both led by the hostess.

PROMOTION DAY PARTY

Besid the annual birthday party, growing children are confirmed in their milestones toward growing up by the annual Sunday school promotion day each Fall. The importance of this day may be increased by the planning of a promotion day party in the primary department. Although parents often attend parties of the kindergarten age children, it is important especially to invite the parents to this occasion. Also teachers and supervisors of the primary department should be extended an invitation.

Decorations

The extent and type of decoration used for this party will depend somewhat on where it is held. However, the general theme of graduation including caps and gowns is appropriate.

Things to Do

(1) *London bridge.* An action game which older kindergarten children love is "London Bridge Is Falling Down." Two children face each other forming a bridge with their arms extended above their heads. All of the other children march under the bridge while the group sings the song, "London Bridge Is Falling Down." On the last note of the song, the two children drop their arms, thereby collapsing the bridge around one of the children who is caught in the center. The game continues until every child has been caught.

(2) *Children's slides.* Children love to see themselves projected in pictures on the screen. If the hostess can secure colored slides or movies showing the boys and girls who are attending the party, the children will be excited beyond measure.

(3) *Shadows.* After the slides or movies have been shown, give the children an opportunity to make shadows on the screen with their fingers.

(4) *Graduation exercise.* If a regular graduation is planned by the Sunday school department, the party may become an informal practice session. Make a production of the children wearing their caps and gowns to receive the promotion certificates which graduate them from the kindergarten and admit them to the primary department.

Refreshments

Graduation cap made of chocolate covered graham cracker placed on top of a freshly frosted chocolate cupcakes
Orange Kool-aid
(Coffee for adults)

Devotions

Since parents will be attending this party, ask two or three of them to pray short prayers for the children who are being promoted.

GRANDMOTHERS' TEA

A very enjoyable event for both children and adults is a grandmothers' tea. The room may be set with folding tables seating two grandmothers and two children at each table. Regular size cups are set for the grandmothers and small demitasse cups for the children. Tea is served to the grandmothers and punch to the boys and girls.

Decorations

The only decorations needed for this party are table centerpieces made of fresh seasonal flowers. Soft background music may be played during most of the tea time.

Things to Do

(1) *Pictures.* Ask each grandmother to bring pictures of her grandchildren which may be shown to other grandmothers present. If it seems appropriate the children may be asked to bring a picture of something they love such as a pet, their home, parents, church, or grandparents. Identifying names should be written on the back of each picture.

(2) *Gift corsages.* Small bouquets of flowers or corsages may be presented by the children to each of the grandmothers. These flowers may be either provided by the hostess or planned for in advance by the boys and girls.

(3) *Ribbon-cutting race.* The children will enjoy the activity of the grandparents in this race. Long pieces of ribbon attached to the wall are placed into the hands of each grandmother along with a pair of scissors. The grandmothers are to cut the ribbon in one continuous line from the beginning to the end. The grandmother who cuts the full length of her ribbon first is the winner. In each instance the grandchild will be an assistant to the grandmother.

(4) *Treasure chest.* A small little box is provided for each child. Coins or foil-wrapped chocolate mints are hidden about the room. The children are asked to find these coins which are then kept in their little box as souvenirs of the party. If it seems appropriate the grandmothers may be asked in advance to bring the decorative little boxes to be presented to their own grandchild for the treasure hunt.

Refreshments

Assorted tea cookies	
Tea	Punch

Devotions

Plan for three tandem-prayers. Three sets of grandmothers and grandchildren will be chosen in advance to lead devotional prayers at the close of the afternoon tea.

A FIREMAN'S PARTY

Since all boys and girls are especially intrigued by firemen and fire engines, this party theme may prove popular among the kindergarten set. Many of the children may have fire engines and other equipment which they may be asked to bring with them.

Decorations

A combination of garden hose, ladders, and bright red colors may be used to decorate for this party.

Things to Do

(1) *Fire truck ride.* If the location and circumstances are right, it may be that arrangements can be made for the children to visit a fire station and even have a ride on a real fire engine.

(2) *Climb the ladder.* Fairly short step ladders may be used to enliven a fireman's race. Most of the children will be overjoyed at the idea of climbing a ladder (with adult supervision, of course).

(3) *Ping pong blow.* The children may each be given a ping pong ball to represent a fire truck. On a given signal they are asked to get their truck to the scene of the fire as soon as possible. (A doll house with red cellophane paper crushed and sticking out the windows is a good prop.) The difficult part is that each child is to *blow* the ping pong ball along the floor to the designated "fire."

(4) *Fireman's hat.* If possible, secure through your Texaco dealer or Fire Safety Office a set of firemen's hats to be given to the boys and girls.

(5) *Blow out the fire.* Give each child an opportunity to play fireman by blowing out an eight-inch candle.

(6) *Free time.* Children this age will occupy themselves well on the theme of the fireman if they can have a few toys and some free time under adult supervision.

Refreshments

Cinnamon apples
Crackers with cheese spread
Red Kool-aid

Devotions

Tell or read the story of Elijah on Mount Carmel as recorded in I Kings 18:1-40.

JINGLE BELLS CHRISTMAS PARTY

Christmas bells, especially those which jingle, make an appropriate theme for kindergarten children at a Christmas party. From construction paper make Christmas bells which will serve as name tags for each child. These may be decorated with an actual pair of small bells.

Decorations

With Christmas music for a background, decorate the room with traditional Christmas objects especially emphasizing the bell. A string of real or artificial sleigh bells which the children may ring will add interest to the party for the boys and girls.

Things to Do

(1) *Christmas chains.* A paper Christmas chain may be made by each child to take home as a decoration in his own room or on the family Christmas tree.

(2) *Jingle bells.* If enough jingle bells can be located, the children will enjoy singing rhythmic Christmas songs to their own accompaniment of bells.

(3) *Gift exchange.* The children may exchange gifts with each other. If this does not seem appropriate the teacher or hostess may want to present each child with a gift from herself. To help drive home a Christmas lesson, these gifts may be distributed by persons in the costumes of the three wise men.

(4) *Tree decorations.* A small tree may be decorated by the boys and girls. The decorations may be made by the children themselves during the party and in previous Sunday school handwork sessions.

(5) *Christmas pieces.* If the boys and girls of the kindergarten department are involved in the annual Christmas program, they may enjoy reciting again the pieces assigned them for the Christmas service.

(6) *Christmas drama.* Some aspect of the total Christmas story may be dramatized by the boys and girls under the direction of the teacher or hostess. The story of the shepherds, the birth of Jesus, the visit of the wise men or the flight of Mary and Joseph to Egypt may be adaptable episodes for this purpose.

Refreshments

Fancy ice cream molds
or
Raspberry jello
Bell-shaped cookies
Strawberry soda pop

Devotions

The teacher or hostess may use her own judgment in the matter of choosing a part of the Christmas story for the devotional period. The account in Luke 2:1-39 of the birth of Jesus, or the story of the wise men in Matthew 2 are especially appropriate. Colored slides and filmstrips are available in many Sunday schools and libraries to be used as visual aids in this type of a devotional.

III. Party Ideas for Primary Children

INDIAN POW-WOW

Both boys and girls of primary age will enjoy an Indian party. Children of this age have an uninhabited imagination, therefore it is important to provide realistic Indian symbols but be certain not to frighten the children. The length of this party probably should be held to one-and-a-half hours. Children should be encouraged to wear Indian costumes or at least to paint their faces.

Decorations

A wigwam centerpiece, feather headdresses, Indian symbols on the wall, and tom-toms made from oatmeal boxes will help create the Indian party atmosphere. Quick costumes may be made from old pillowcases: cut out a neck on the sewn end, arm holes on each side, and fringe the "shirt" on the bottom. The children can decorate these with crayon in Indian designs.

Things to Do

(1) *Indian names.* When each child arrives assign him an Indian name. Chief Big Sky, Princess Laughing-Brook, Chief Bald-Eagle, Chief Thundercloud, Princess Fire-Maker, are a few suggestions.

(2) *Construct wigwams.* From small slender sticks and brown wrapping paper, each child may construct his own tepee for a souvenir of the day. The poles for the tepee should be twelve to eighteen inches high. Three poles are needed for each tepee. The brown paper may be brightly colored in Indian style.

(3) *Headdresses.* On arrival present each child with an Indian headdress. These may be bought quite economically or can be constructed to the degree of finesse your resources and time will permit. Crepe paper may be used for the head band. Cut the strips across the grain, four by twenty inches. Fold lengthwise and paste the end of the feathers across the front of the head band in the fold. Use scotch tape to fasten each headdress on the children. They must fit individually.

(4) *Story time.* The children will love the section of Longfellow's "Hiawatha" on Hiawatha's childhood. Also the story of Captain John Smith and the Indian Maiden Pocahontas will be most appropriate.

(5) *Wampum.* For Indian money give the children a bag of candy corn and short flat licorice strips.

(6) *Stick horse race.* Imaginary Indian ponies may be constructed from broom handles or from pieces of wood about one inch square and three feet long.

(7) *Construct Indian drums.* Secure a quantity of oatmeal or other round boxes. Cover the sides with paper which has been decorated with

Indian symbols. The ends may be colored with crayons.

(8) *"One little, two little, three little Indians."* Children skip in a circle singing, "One little, two little, three little Indians." Choose one spot on the floor where a big circle is drawn to represent an Indian trap. When the song is ended the children stop skipping. The child standing at the marked place steps into the center of the circle. The final person to escape the trap is the winner.

(9) *Indian drawing contest.* Supply paper and crayons for the children to draw scenes from Indian stories or pictures of Indians. Offer a prize for the best picture voted by the children.

(10) *Cowboys and Indians.* Allow the children free time to play their own game of Cowboys and Indians. They will know the rules!

Refreshments

Corn bread muffins *
Assorted fresh fruit tray
Apple juice

Devotions

Develop brief devotions by using the following religious symbols of early Indians: (1) White man's book of heaven (Bible), (2) Happy hunting ground (Heaven), (3) Great tepee (church), (4) The Great White Father (God), (5) Spirit messages (prayer). Ask the children to join hands while singing a closing chorus, "Into My Heart." Conclude with prayer.

* See Party Recipes section in back of book.

COWBOY PARTY

There is nothing an All-American primary age boy enjoys more than a party completely dedicated to the theme of the American cowboy. And don't underestimate the girls. They like cowboys too. Urge the children to dress as cowboys complete with side arms, sheriff badges, and boots.

Decorations

The place of the party will fairly well dictate the type of decorations which can be used. Some of the following things will help to create a western atmosphere if they are available and appropriate: bales of hay, nail kegs, corral fence, saddle, horseshoes, ten gallon hats, and heavy ropes.

Things to Do

(1) *Costumes.* If the children have been urged to wear their costumes, plan a costume judging contest at the very beginning of the party. Give several prizes.

(2) *Pictures.* Grandparents, parents, and even the children themselves will cherish any pictures you are able to take at this cowboy party. Color slides, black and white still pictures, and movies are all appropriate according to your resources.

(3) *Stage coach.* While the children are all seated, assign each of them the name of one particular part of the stage coach such as the seat, harness, brake, hub, driver, baggage, horses, tire, door, or step. The sponsor of the party will begin to tell an involved story which mentions all of the various parts of the stage coach. It may be well to have this story written out in advance. As each item is mentioned the player or players representing it gets up and runs around his own chair. At an unexpected moment in the story the teller shouts, Stage coach!" which is the signal for everyone to exchange seats with someone else. The storyteller tries to get a seat in the scramble and thus leaves another player to begin a new story. (This game could be adapted for the story of Abraham sending his servant to secure a wife for Isaac.)

(4) *Hide and Seek.* All of the children hide except *It* who looks for them. If a player gets back to home base without being seen he is "home free." The last one to get back to home base without being seen, or the first one *It* catches is then *It* for the next game.

(5) *Rabbit and dog.* Players stand in a circle. One bean bag to represent the rabbit and another to represent the dog are given to players on opposite sides of the circle. When the signal is given they start passing the rabbit and the dog from one

person to another as fast as they can around the circle to the right. The idea of the game is for the dog to catch the rabbit. If the rabbit completes three trips around the circle without being caught he is declared safe.

(6) *Free time.* Allow the children ample time of their own. They may want to play cowboys and Indians or other games which they particularly enjoy.

(7) *Hat contest.* Place a ten gallon hat in the middle of a circle and let the children compete with each other trying to throw a ping pong ball into it.

(8) *Pony rides.* If resources are available, the cowboy party will be long remembered if actual pony rides can be arranged.

(9) *Outside cooking.* If the weather and circumstances permit, a grand closing can be made for the cowboy party by outdoor cooking. If possible this should be done over an open fire rather than on a modern, up-to-date grill.

Refreshments

    Chuck wagon hamburgers
        Potato chips
    Soda pop, assorted flavors

Devotions

In the book of Genesis there is a most thrilling story about Abraham and his nephew Lot who had herdsmen who quarreled with each other. This probably is the first wild-west story in the world. Abraham and Lot finally divided their territory because of the quarreling herdsmen. Read this story from the Bible, read it from one of the Bible story book versions, or tell it yourself. Plan closing prayers which express thanks to God for the great out-of-doors.

PIRATE PARTY

Although this party will be especially enjoyable for boys, girls also will be glad to become pirates for a day. Invitations may be written on black construction paper using white ink.

Decorations

Red and green pennants may be flying both outside and inside the house. At least one pennant should have on it a skull and crossbones. Red and green lightbulbs may be used for atmosphere. A wooden treasure chest on the table, black paper chains hanging on hooks or doorknobs, and a pair of binoculars may help to add to the decorations.

A twelve-inch plank may be spread between two kitchen step ladders as a real pirate's entrance into the party area. A black table cloth may be used on a picnic table decorated with red paper napkins. Use aluminum foil plates (the kind TV dinners come in).

A centerpiece for the refreshment table may be made with a piece of aluminum foil crumpled and then spread out fairly smooth in the center of the table. On top of this place a layer of dark blue cellophane which has been crushed. Over the cellophane place a layer of light green cellophane which has been crushed also. These will represent the ocean waves. In the center there may be placed a model of a pirate ship.

Things to Do

(1) *Judge costumes.*

(2) *Treasure chest.* Almost any restaurant supply house has an inexpensive assortment of candy and trinkets complete with a sturdy cardboard treasure chest. If one of these can be bought, it will serve as the source for all prizes during the party. Each winner in turn will be allowed to choose his own gift from the treasure chest.

(3) *Catch the pirate.* While the children are standing in a circle, the pirate who has been chosen *It* walks around the outside of the circle slowly with a blood-red handkerchief dangling from the tips of his fingers. Behind an unsuspecting child he drops the handkerchief and begins to run. The child picks up the handkerchief and runs in the opposite direction trying to beat the pirate back to his own spot. If he fails, then this child becomes the pirate with the blood-red handkerchief.

(4) *Walk the plank.* When ancient pirate captains wanted to give their captives a chance to save their lives, they were asked to walk a long springy plank extended from the deck of the ship out over the ocean. The victim was blindfolded and asked to

walk out to the end of the plank and back again. If he were able to do this his life was saved. For this game use a twelve foot plank about twelve inches wide placed flat on the ground. You may make this as realistic as you feel is appropriate according to the ages of the children and the circumstances.

(5) *Pirate, save my life.* Dress up one of the children complete with an eye patch and rubber knife. Each of the children in turn kneels in front of the pirate and calls out, "Pirate, pirate, save my life." The pirate then makes all kinds of motions and sound in an effort to cause the victim to laugh or smile. If he can make them laugh or smile, their life is then lost and they become the pirate.

(6) *Frozen handshake.* Prepare a rubber glove filled with ice and kept in a deep freeze until hard. During the game each boy is blindfolded and asked to shake hands with the frozen hand.

(7) *Seaweed hunt.* For a really eerie pirate experience, prepare a large bowl of cooked noodles. Hide pennies in the noodles. Blindfold each boy individually while he searches through the seaweed to find himself a penny.

(8) *Film.* Your local library may have a pirate film suitable for showing the children.

Refreshments

Pierce a popsicle stick through a hot dog. Attach with toothpicks a triangular slice of cheese to form the pirate's hat. Make features and decorations with pieces of ripe and green olives. Serve with bread and butter sandwiches and grape Kool-aid.

Devotions

Dr. Luke in the book of Acts gives a marvelous account of the shipwreck of the Apostle Paul. This story may be read or told to the children in the closing devotional moments of the party.

DOLL PARTY

This party is especially adapted for the birthday of a little girl. Although it is planned only for children, it would not be out of order to have mothers or grandmothers attend the party with the little girls. The girls should arrive with their own dolls wrapped in blankets and even tucked in a toy stroller or baby carriage. Much of the party time will be used in independent play.

Decorations

Both small and large dolls may be used to decorate the party room. It will take only a little imagination to build a decorative centerpiece using a small doll as the main object.

Things to Do

(1) *Sew.* The hostess should provide needles, thread, scissors, and fabrics and trimmings for the girls to use in making doll clothes. This is especially appropriate if the mothers have come with the girls. The mothers may even have portable sewing machines available.

(2) *Make cookies.* Every girl may not enjoy sewing. Some may work with their mothers in the preparation of cookies for the entire group.

(3) *Show and tell.* In turn ask each child to show her own doll and tell something about her. There probably is a special reason why one particular doll is her favorite and was chosen to bring to the doll party.

(4) *Keep away.* For an active game, place the children in a fair-sized circle with one of them in the center. Use an old Raggedy Ann doll which will be tossed from one child to another in an effort to "keep away" from the child in the center. As soon as the child in the center is able to retrieve the doll, then the last person who tossed it exchanges places.

(5) *Magazine hunt.* With plenty of magazines, scissors, paste, and paper at hand, the girls may enjoy searching for attractive pictures to paste in a scrapbook provided by the hostess. The scrapbook might be planned for a hospitalized child.

Refreshments

    Doll cake*
    Cambric tea*

Devotions

While St. Paul was visiting the church in Philippi he became acquainted with a business woman by the name of Lydia. She became famous in the Bible as a dealer in expensive purple dye. Since girls are interested in colors, an interesting and helpful devotional may be built around Lydia and her business. After you have read the Scriptural passage to the girls, then talk to them briefly about Lydia on the basis of the information you have gained from reading your own Bible dictionary and commentary.

* See Party Recipes section in back of book.

PUMPKIN PARTY

Boys and girls of primary age love a Hallowe'en party. However, there is a danger in making it a frightening experience for them unless some restraint is exercised in planning the evening. In fact, it may be best to hold the party in the afternoon or at least in the early hours after the evening meal. Invitations may be made by cutting jack-o'-lantern faces from orange construction paper.

Decorations

A Hallowe'en table must be highly decorative. Cover the table first with orange crepe paper and then place a strip of black crepe paper as a runner down the center. In the center place a pumpkin jack-o'-lantern with a lighted candle. Alongside the pumpkin, place black cat figures. Witches cut from black paper may be pinned on the draperies in the room. A miniature skeleton may be hung from the chandelier over the table.

Things to Do

(1) *Pass the pumpkin.* Everyone stands in a circle before their chairs. As music is played a small pumpkin is passed from hand to hand. Music stops at intervals and the one holding the pumpkin must sit down. The one left standing last is the winner.

(2) *Trick or treat.* Prepare a paper bag with many slips of paper in it. On some of the slips will be written, "treat," on other, "trick." Pass the bag around while music is played. When the music stops the one holding the paper bag pulls out one slip of paper. If he pulls out treat, he will be presented with a piece of candy. But if he pulls out trick he will be assigned a stunt to perform.

(3) *Hunting witches.* Before the guests arrive cut a dozen little black witches out of construction paper and hide around the room. Each person is given a small plastic bag to hold his witches. Children are asked to find as many of the witches as they can. Present the winning person with a cookie or candy witch.

(4) *The cat's tail.* This is a search for the cat's tail. If possible have a large figure of a black cat on a piece of cardboard which is constructed to expose the ends of three pieces of bright colored yarn. The pieces of yarn are carefully hidden with a short end of each showing. The children are given turns choosing which piece of yarn is the actual tail of the cat. The pieces of yarn they choose may turn out to be an inch or a foot long. Those who choose the cat's real tail receive prizes.

(5) *Jack-o'-lantern drawing contest.* Give each child a large sheet

of paper and a supply of crayons. Allow him ample time to create his own jack-o'-lantern picture. After the children have voted on the best jack-o'-lantern, present the winner with a prize.

(6) *Cinderella's shoe.* At a given signal each girl takes off her right shoe and throws it into a pile in the center of the room. At another signal each boy picks a shoe from the pile to find the girl to whom it belongs. The winner is the boy who can find his Cinderella first.

(7) *Doughnut faces.* Type out Hallowe'en fortunes on small pieces of thin paper and roll them to fit into the hole of a doughnut. Cover the hole with a black gumdrop. Then to complete a pumpkin face make eyes of cloves and a mouth of a gumdrop which has been cut lengthwise. The ears will also be made of half gumdrops fastened with toothpicks. Each child may examine his "Hallowe'en fortune" and then eat the funny face.

Refreshments

Doughnut faces
(See number seven — Things to Do)
Cold apple cider

Devotions

Secure a good but brief story like the ones often printed in Sunday school papers for small children. Hollow out a small pumpkin and place the story inside. Leave this pumpkin in plain sight for the party but do not refer to it. When time has come for devotions use a large butcher knife to cut open the pumpkin. It may appear to the children that you are opening it for the first time. They will find great delight in the fact that a story is lodged on the inside. Read the story and then close the party time with prayer.

EASTER EGG PARTY

This type party is especially appealing to children from four to ten years of age. The charming old tradition of hiding Easter eggs for children is again growing in popularity. The most logical time for this party is on Saturday afternoon before Easter. In the morning before the party, hide the Easter eggs in a given area. If weather does not permit an outside Easter egg hunt, then do the next best by hiding them indoors.

For invitations, a series of six Easter eggs may be cut from construction paper, stacked together, and stapled. Write a portion of your invitation on each of the eggs.

Decorations

Use a large table with a cloth which comes almost to the ground. Pin many colored paper eggs and bunny rabbits onto the portion of the cloth which is hanging. Center the table with a large stuffed Easter bunny sitting in a nest of green excelsior.

Things to Do

(1) *Easter egg hunt.* Your Easter egg hunt may be made a little more interesting by adding to your traditional eggs a few extra eggs made from styrofoam, candy eggs wrapped in foil and one "golden" egg in gold foil. Explain in advance that special prizes will be given to those who find these special eggs. Provide small baskets for the children to use in collecting the eggs they find. It does no harm for mothers or older brother and sisters to be on hand to offer guidance to the children especially if they are small. Each child should be allowed to take home the basket of eggs he finds.

(2) *Easter cards.* Provide gummed stars, dots, little gold decals, sequins, strips of gummed gold paper, tiny paper butterflies, colored gummed tape, and cement. Also several small scissors, crayons, magic markers, and wide strips of construction paper will be needed for the children to make imaginative Easter cards to give to friends and family.

(3) *Egg running contest.* Divide guests into two teams for a relay. Give each player a teaspoon with instructions to hold it by the handle between his teeth. The first member of each team has a styrofoam or plastic egg placed in the bowl of his spoon. On the signal the team members walk across the room and back again keeping their hands clasped behind their back, without dropping the egg. Each team member takes his turn until every person on the relay team has successfully run the race. The team finishing first is declared winner.

(4) *Egg roll.* The boys compete with each other by rolling a hard-

boiled egg from the starting to the finishing line with the use of their nose only.

(5) *Coloring eggs.* If circumstances are right, the children may find a great deal of joy in coloring the Easter eggs prior to their hunt.

Refreshments
Assorted crackers
Colored deviled eggs
Celery and carrot sticks
White cupcakes with
coconut covered pastel frostings
Lemon-lime Kool-aid

Devotions
Since the idea of Easter eggs and bunnies is from the ancient festival of spring and not from the resurrection story of Jesus, it is important to conclude the Easter egg hunt with devotions which clearly explain the difference to the children. Perhaps the pastor can do this. Or, it may be good to have four of the older children read in turn from Matthew's gospel those verses which refer to 1) the betrayal by Judas, 2) the death of Jesus on the cross, 3) His resurrection, and 4) the ascension.

AIRPLANE PARTY

In this day of air travel, boys and girls will enjoy a party planned around the theme of an airplane. Envelopes from the local airline office may be used for sending the invitations. It is likely the airlines also will provide cards with a picture of a large airplane on one side and space for the party invitation on the other.

Decorations

Secure from the airlines company, posters, flight wings, caps, and other materials which are adaptable for use at a children's party. A toy airplane may be used for special decoration on the table. Build a runway down the center of the table complete with toy buildings and air tower. Place the plane on the runway.

Things to Do

(1) *Show planes*. Many boys have collections of airplanes. One of the boys may be asked to bring his collection to show and explain to the others. Or it may be that several boys may bring one plane each.

(2) *A pretend airplane ride*. The entire party may be built around the idea of setting up chairs to emulate the inside of a jet. Although the children may leave their seats at various landings to play games they will always return to the seat which was assigned them before takeoff. Refreshments may be served on trays and eaten at the seats.

(3) *Film*. Both airline companies and the public library are good sources to secure excellent films on air travel or flying. These may be viewed by the children as they sit in their "airplane seats" in the party room.

(4) *Fly away*. Stand the children in a semi-circle and appoint a leader from among the older boys and girls. The leader spreads out his arms as if they were wings and calls the name of a number of different things such as ducks, robins, pigeons, airplanes, and geese. Intermittently, the leader, while still flapping his wings, will mention something that does not fly. He will say "dogs fly." If any child waves his arms at something that does not fly, he must drop out of the game.

(5) *Radar*. One child is chosen pilot of the plane. He leaves the room while the rest hide an object which he must find on his return. The closer he comes to the object the more the children clap. The pilot should know what the object is before he leaves the room. The clapping radar should help him find it on his return.

(6) *Airport visit*. If you live near a commercial airport, arrangements probably can be made for the boys and girls not only to visit the airport but actually to go inside a larger plane.

(7) *Favors*. Tiny airplanes may be formed from two sticks of chewing gum. One forms the body of the

plane, the other the wings. Attach together with a rubber band on which you have strung two mint lifesavers. The mints are the "wheels."

(8) *Build model plane.* Perhaps some of the children at the party will enjoy constructing a model plane during the progress of the party.

(9) *Pennies from heaven.* If you have an upper deck or second story window, ask the children to gather in an area below where you will throw handfuls of pennies. Give each child a small nylon net bag for collecting the pennies he can find on the ground.

Refreshments

Use a sectional aluminum foil plate. Serve a sandwich in one section, a fruit cup in one section, and potato chips in the third. Serve Kool-aid in substantial paper cups.

Devotions

The most exciting air ride in history was taken by the prophet Elijah in a chariot of fire. This story is not only recorded in the Bible but written in modern language in several Bible story books. It will be an excellent basis for the closing devotions at an airplane party for primary children.

FISHING PARTY

The fishing theme offers many good adaptations for a party to intrigue primary age children. Even at this age they are well aware of the great international pastime of matching wits with a fish. Nets, poles and lines, boats, and tackle equipment never cease to be of great interest to young and old.

Decorations

A large gold fish bowl may make a good centerpiece on the table. The room may be decorated with pictures of fish, the ocean, rivers, and lakes. Stuffed fish, and even fishing gear may be used on the walls for decorations. These will intrigue the children.

Things to Do

(1) *Fish pond*. There are several ways to set up a fish pond for the boys and girls. They can be given small poles and asked to throw their line over the top of the partition such as a folding screen or sheet strung across the end of the room. A person on the other side will then fasten a small gift to the line which the child retrieves. Or little gifts may be wrapped and tied with ribbons. These are then tagged with strings which are exposed to the side of the children. They choose the string which they will pull and therefore, by chance, catch their gift.

(2) *Fish in the sea*. All players but one stand behind the line. That one is *It* and stands midway between the line behind which the runners are standing and another point some thirty or forty feet away. He shouts:

"Fish in the ocean
Fish in the sea;
Don't get the notion,
You'll get by me."

After this challenge all the fish must leave safety and try to cross to the opposite line without being caught. Players who are caught join hands with *It* (the fisherman) and help form a "net" to catch the others. If the net breaks, players caught on that turn are released.

(3) *Story time*. Ask two or three of the older children who read best to read aloud some of the familiar stories in the Bible which pertain to fish or fishing. Jonah and the whale, Peter and his nets, and the story of Jesus preparing the fish fry in Galilee are possible choices.

(4) *Bean bag toss*. This little game can be very elaborate or plain. The simplest approach is to use a bucket which represents the mouth of a whale. The children may take turns tossing three bean bags each, trying to put them in the whale's mouth. A more elaborate version may involve the cutting of a form of a whale and painting in the fish com-

PARTY IDEAS FOR PRIMARY CHILDREN

plete with open mouth which is used as the object of the bean bag toss.

(5) *Fish stories.* The boys and girls may have stories of their own concerning their personal experiences at fishing. These may prove very interesting.

(6) *Free time.* No party of primary age children will ever go amiss in planning for free time during which the children may develop play as they like.

(7) *Sail boats.* If the circumstances and resources are right, the boys and girls will get great sport out of playing with boats in a tub or play pool.

Refreshments

Tuna fish sandwiches
Ripe olives
Ice cream bars   Punch

Devotions

The 153 fish caught by the disciples is a most interesting story. The story can either be read or told. Apply the lesson of obedience.

TOY PARTY

This party is especially good during January and February. The children's supply of toys is probably greatest at this time of the year. Use white construction paper folded in the middle for each invitation. On the face of the paper, paste the picture of a toy. Ask the children to come and also to bring their favorite toy with them.

Decorations

Decorating for a toy party is fun. Tie extra large ribbons on the toys at hand and place them around the room for decorations. For a centerpiece, use a nice toy such as a large doll or drum. Lots of toy balloons will increase the festive atmosphere. Stuffed animals will also be excellent for decorating a room for a toy party.

Things to Do

(1) *Pre-party time*. As the children arrive, let them go directly to a supply of toys which is available for their entertainment.

(2) *Show and tell*. Ask each child to display his favorite toy received at Christmas. He should be encouraged to allow the other children to examine and play with his toy.

(3) *Live toys*. Pretend the children are toys in a shop. Choose one child to be the storekeeper. Give each child a name such as a doll, a train, car, horn, or drum. When the storekeeper calls the name of one of the toys then the child must stand up and act out the kind of toy he or she is.

(4) *Bible story time*. Certain toys may be reminders of Bible stories or Bible characters. Guide the children in making the connection between these toys and the person or event:

David .... a toy harp
Noah .... an ark with animals
Peter .... a net of fish
Matthew .... a cash register
Lydia ......
   a basket with bits of purple cloth
Martha .. a toy broom or toy dishes
Dorcas .... a small sewing kit
Joseph ......
   a scarf or cloak of many colors
Luke .... a Bible scroll

(5) *The scramble*. The object of this game is to pick up and put into a sack as many articles as possible. The game ends when there is nothing left to pick up. The winner is the child who has collected the most. Such things as lollipops, peanuts, pennies and candy kisses, may be gathered. A paper bag or plastic sack should be furnished each contestant.

(6) *"I see a toy."* This is a good game to quiet the children. Ask the children to sit in a circle. Then say to the children, "I am thinking about a particular toy; what is it?" The children may ask questions about the object until they guess what it is.

The toy you are thinking about should be in plain sight of the children.

(7) *Fun on the farm.* The children are seated in a circle. Each one chooses to be some farm animal. When everyone has decided what animal he is, you tell a simple story mentioning each of the animals in the course of the tale. When an animal is named the child who has chosen to be that animal must make its sound. If a child says he is a cow, he calls "Moo, Moo" when that animal is mentioned in the story.

(8) *Follow the leader.* The children line up behind the leader who walks along with the children following. They must imitate everything the leader does in the walk. Flapping arms like a bird, hopping on one leg, clapping hands, placing hands on head, and walking and bowing are just a few easy movements children can copy. Each child may take a turn at being leader. It probably is best for the sponsor of the group to be the first leader.

(9) *Free time.*

Refreshments
>Banana boat plate*
>Bread sticks
>Hot cocoa

Devotions

One of the children may have a science set which he can use for presenting an object lesson. Or a flannelgraph or object lesson may be presented by an adult. An imaginative sponsor may be able to improvise an object lesson from the toys which the children have brought with them.

* See Party Recipes section in back of book.

BALLOON PARTY

Since there are many ways to use balloons why not let them be the theme for a primary age party? The invitations, decorations, and most of the games can be built around the idea of balloons. A construction paper balloon complete with string can be used for the invitation.

Things to Do

(1) *Balloon race.* Supply each player with a balloon. As each one's turn comes he must blow up a balloon, race across the room with it and come back again. Then he must sit on it until it breaks. Perhaps it is better to divide into teams so that two persons can be racing at the same time.

(2) *Balloon bursting contest.* A balloon race begins with each child blowing up his own balloon. The first one to blow his balloon until it bursts is the winner. Continue the game until each child has succeeded in bursting his balloon.

(3) *Pussy wants a corner.* It starts around the circle of children who are sitting on chairs or cushions. He says, "Pussy wants a corner," and each child in turn answers, "Please go to my next door neighbor." The children meanwhile try to change places without being caught by the pussy cat.

(4) *Drop the handkerchief.* This well-known game is loved by children of the younger primary age.

(5) *Hot ball.* The children sit in a large circle on the floor. A rubber ball is given to one child. He quickly pushes the ball on to another person as if it were hot. The children try never to hold the ball long because it is "a hot ball." While the ball is being passed music is played. When the music stops, the child with the "hot ball" is out.

(6) *Choose your favor.* Place as many favors as there are children on a long table or sidewalk. These favors will consist of a variety of small toys or candies. Line up the children at some distance from the favors. When the signal is given they race to secure their particular favor. It is much more fun for primary age children to race for the favor than to have it handed to them.

(7) *Hopping contest.* Let the children see how well and how far they can hop. Offer a prize to the child who can hop the longest period of time.

(8) *A take-home surprise.* Give each child an inflated balloon mounted on a stick or tied with a piece of string. Attach the stick or string to a little package which the child is not to open until arriving home. The packages may consist of such things as crayons, chocolate bars, or chewing gum.

Refreshments

To make balloon sandwiches, use pastel tinted bread. Spread with your favorite fillings and cut with a large biscuit cutter. Pass platter of colorful balloon sandwiches. Serve with cold milk and wrapped candies.

Devotions

Read or tell the story of Jesus when He was twelve years of age at the temple in Jerusalem. Then give a two minute devotional on how He grew: 1) in stature, 2) in favor with God, 3) in favor with man.

GROWN-UP TEA PARTY

Ask the little girls to dress up in mother's old hats, high-heeled shoes, and purses which they have brought from home. They will wear these throughout the party. Playing grown-up will be enough entertainment in itself. Floral notepaper may be used for writing the invitations. If it seems appropriate, mothers may also be asked to attend this party with their little girls.

Decorations

The tea tables constitute the decorations for this party. Use low children's tables and children's chairs. Cover the tables with fancy tablecloths. Centerpieces of flowers should be used. Fruit tea should be served in china cups.

Things to Do

(1) *Free time.* Provide the girls with plenty of free time for make-believe play.

(2) *"What am I?"* Write the name of a simple familiar object on a tag. Examples: cat, dog, fish, apple, and tree. Pin a tag on the back of each guest. The children try to find out what they are by asking each other questions. Such questions take the form of "Am I red?" or "Can I fly?" and must be answered by yes or no only. The first child to guess what he is wins the prize. However, the game should continue until every child has guessed his identity.

(3) *Milk bottle contest.* Give each girl five wooden clothespins. She is asked to drop the pins in an empty milk bottle which is placed on the floor. She may kneel facing the back of a chair and hold her arms on the top of the chair as she steadies her fingers for dropping the clothespins. Give the child with the highest score a prize.

(4) *Rainbow prize.* Little girls will enjoy following the rainbow to the pot of gold. The rainbow will consist of long pieces of ribbon which are tied to a chocolate wrapped in gold foil. The girls follow the pieces of ribbon to the point where the gold is hidden.

(5) *Paper hat making.* As the children arrive, send them to a table where the necessary materials are available for making their own hats. Old hats make a good base to be decorated. Paper can also be folded and trimmed. Feathers, beads, ribbons, rick-rack, scotch tape, glue, large needles and thread will all make interesting and helpful materials with which to work.

(6) *Ribbon cutting contest.* Provide each child with a one-inch wide

paper streamer eight feet long. Give each girl a pair of small scissors. On a given signal each girl will begin to cut her streamer lengthwise. The first one who succeeds in cutting her streamer in half from one end to the other is the winner. Any contestant who cuts through the edge of her streamer is disqualified.

* See Party Recipes section in back of book.

Refreshments
Fruit tea*
Assorted tea cookies
Mints

Devotions
Make a few appropriate comments on Genesis 9:12 for closing devotions. God's promises are still true.

CHILDREN'S CHRISTMAS PARTY

Every child looks forward to the Christmas party planned by his Sunday school teacher or department supervisor. This is the happiest time of the year for children of this age. Many variations can be made on the Christmas theme. The suggestions that are made here will not be appropriate for all groups in all places.

Decorations

The traditional Christmas tree is probably the best kind of decoration for primary age children. Although there is difference of opinion among people, many feel it is best not to promote the idea of Santa Claus but rather to emphasize the manger. If a creche is available, it may be used both for decorations and closing devotions.

Things to Do

(1) *Lollipop faces.* Help the children make lollipop clowns. Have the ingredients on a table before the guests arrive. Cover a lollipop with white paper and paint a face on it. Then using wax paper to make the hole in the doughnut smaller, stick the doughnut up to the base of the lollipop. Place the lollipop stick into a styrofoam ball cut in half. Place a paper clown hat on the lollipop head. Names of the children may be written with a felt pen marker on the styrofoam base.

(2) *Gum-drop figures.* Place a number of gum-drops of various sizes, shapes, and colors in a large bowl. Ask the children to sit around tables to work and supply them with toothpicks for use in making figures. Also they must have cloves to use as eyes and perhaps tiny marshmallows and raisins for added decoration on their figures. They may either take home or eat on the spot the results of their handiwork.

(3) *Christmas nut-eating contest.* Divide the children into teams. Seat them on the floor at opposite ends of the room. Give each child ten Christmas nuts in shells. Each youngster must shell the nuts he has and eat them. The team who finishes first is declared the winner. Several nutcrackers or small hammers and a board should be provided for the contest.

(4) *Kangaroo tag.* This lively form of tag played by Australian youngsters is an invitation for players of other nations to "hop to it." The children must keep their feet together and hop while they play this game of tag. A player who fails to do this is ruled out.

(5) *Christmas orange contest.* Divide the guests into two teams. At the signal the first person in each line pushes an orange to the far wall using a pencil. Then he returns to the

head of the line using the pencil to push the orange back. The next player does the same thing. The first team to finish wins.

(6) *Pin star on tree.* Pin a child's tempera painting of a large Christmas tree on the wall. Each player is blindfolded and given a turn at pinning an aluminum foil star on top of the tree. Clap for the winner.

(7) *Jingle bells.* The children form a large circle around two players who are called Mr. and Mrs. Jingle Bells. Mrs. Jingle Bells is blindfolded and Mr. Jingle Bells carries a small bell that tinkles when he moves. It is tied to his shoelace. When Mrs. Jingle Bells catches him she takes his place and another player becomes the one looking for the bell.

(8) *Christmas program.* The children may enjoy a short impromptu Christmas program which involves the repeating of the numbers they have prepared for the annual Christmas Sunday school program.

(9) *Film on Christmas.* There is an endless number of wonderful Christmas films available in both slide, filmstrip, and movie form. These may be shown while refreshments are being prepared.

Refreshments

  Fruited cherry jello molds
    Whipped cream
   Finger sandwiches
   Chocolate cupcakes
  Fruit punch poured over
    orange sherbert

Devotions

While the room is illuminated only by the candles and the Christmas tree lights, read the story of Christmas to the boys and girls. Then contrast the real meaning of Christmas with the commercial emphasis the children feel outside the church and home. Ask several children to lead in Christmas prayers. The children may join hands and close devotions by singing, "O Little Town of Bethlehem."

SPRING TIME PARTY

Children love the coming of spring. After being confined through the winter months, they will find reason to celebrate the first signs of spring. This party may be planned indoors or out, according to weather conditions. However, the games should all be active and substantial refreshments should be planned.

Decorations

The children may cut out leaves from green construction paper. Bird and flower pictures may be cut from magazines. Decorate the room or patio with the cutouts. Real flowers may also be used if available.

Things to Do

(1) *Red Rover*. This is a game which can be played when the children are all about the same age and size, and if the weather permits outdoor activity. Two captains choose teams with an equal number of players. They join hands, making two lines which face each other about sixty feet apart. The captain of one side calls, "Red rover, red rover, send 'someone' right over." The "someone" whose name they have just called then leaves his side and races toward the other. The object is to break through the human chain. If he succeeds he is allowed to return to his side and take one member of the opposite team with him. If he fails to break through he must stay with the opposing side and add to their chain. This continues with the captains calling, "Red rover" alternately until only one person is left on the losing side.

(2) *Statue tag*. In statue tag *It* tries to tag the other players. If they get into a statue pose before being tagged, they are safe.

Stoop tag is a variation. In order to keep from being tagged by *It* the player may stoop as soon as *It* is ready to tag him. Any player tagged who is not stooping becomes *It*.

Touch tag is another variation. When *It* tags another player, that child becomes *It* and must put one hand over the part of his body which was touched. He must do this until he tags someone else.

(3) *London Bridge*. Two players hold their joined hands as high as they can forming an arch representing a bridge. The two players agree between them what each is representing, a rose or lily, a pearl or diamond, a crown or silver slippers, but they do not let the other players know. Players march around in a circle, then through the arch while singing the song. On the words, "my fair lady," the bridge comes down on some player. The two children forming the bridge whisper to the captured,

"Which would you rather be, a lily or a rose?" The child makes his choice. Not until then does he know which side he will go on. The player stands behind the one he has chosen and the game continues until each child has become a victim of the bridge. The game can end in a tug-of-war between the two teams.

(4) *Pussy wants a corner.* All the players except one occupy chairs or stand with hands against a tree or post. The player who is It goes around to each of the others saying, "Pussy wants a corner." The reply from the player is, "Go to my next door neighbor." Any two players may signal one another and make an exchange of corners. When they do, pussy tries to get into one of the places. If he is successful, the player who is left out becomes the pussy.

(5) *Tight rope walking.* Stretch three lengths of white tape each twelve feet long across the room parallel to one another. These represent tightropes. Choose three contestants who stand with both feet on the tape, one foot in front of the other. Give each of the guests a pair of opera glasses and tell him to focus them on his tightrope. At the signal to start they are to race to the ends of the tightrope. The only rules are, first, that they may not take their eyes away from the large lenses of the glasses; and second, that they must not step off the tape.

(6) *Bug race.* The children race, running on their hands and feet, not their knees. Only the "bugs" who run the entire race on their hands and feet are qualified to be a winner.

(7) *Lame wolf.* One player is chosen as the lame wolf. All of the other players are the children. A space is marked off for the wolf's den. At the other end of the playing space a house is marked off for the children. After the wolf goes to his den the children run out of the house and begin to taunt the wolf singing, "Who's afraid of the big bad wolf?" When the wolf thinks he has a good chance to catch someone he dashes out of his den in pursuit. However, he can only run three steps when he must start hopping on one foot. Anyone caught becomes a lame wolf and must help catch the other children. When all of the children are safe at home, the wolf and his mates retire to their den waiting for the children to come forth again with their taunts.

Refreshments

Small sandwiches
Strawberry ice cream cones
Angel food cake
Strawberry Kool-aid

Devotions

One of the most appropriate Scripture passages for a spring party is the parable of the sower. It is likely Jesus was sitting with His disciples on a hillside when He looked across the way to a man broadcasting seed in a nearby field. He made His sermon from the subject at hand. After reading or telling the story to the children you may make applications which they can understand about the planting of a spring garden.

MOTHER'S DAY PARTY

The weekend of Mother's Day is an excellent time to plan a party honoring the mothers of the primary age children. These youngsters are not yet self-conscious about their mothers. They will rally to the idea of a party in mother's honor. It may be appropriate to plan this as a luncheon.

Decorations

Let the children follow their own suggestions in decorations for the Mother's Day party. There is an ample supply of poster material which they may want to use. Also, corsages should be made and presented to the mothers as they arrive at the party. Perhaps the children will want to make their own place cards. For a small expenditure, the words, "I love you," may be made from styrofoam and used in the center of the table.

Things to Do

(1) *Charades*. The mothers of the Bible may be used as appropriate subjects for charades. Perhaps the mothers will compete against the children in these presentations. A few Bible mothers who may be used for this game are Mary the mother of Jesus, Elizabeth the mother of John the Baptist, Rebecca the mother of Jacob and Esau, and Jochebed the mother of Moses.

(2) *Corsages*. Instead of presenting the corsages to the mothers on their arrival, it may be well to make a ceremony of this presentation. One of the children can make a little speech of appreciation for mothers while all of the boys and girls participate in giving the corsages.

(3) *Grandmothers*. It may be well to invite grandmothers to this special Mother's Day party. If so, they should be given special attention. Maybe individual red roses can be presented to all of the grandmothers present.

(4) *Pictures*. A memorable occasion such as a Mother's Day party should certainly be recorded for future reference. Perhaps a father of one of the children can be the official photographer.

(5) *Stories of famous Bible mothers*. Perhaps one of the grandmothers could be prepared to present two or three stories of famous mothers in the Bible.

(6) *Make gifts for Mother*. If it is not practical for the mothers to be present at the party, the children may want to make gifts which can later be presented to them. Suggestions for gifts include aprons, potholders, laundry bags, paper table mats, and decorated soaps.

(7) *"Why we love Mother."* Several of the children may make very brief speeches on "Why we love Mother."

(8) *Flower guessing game.* This is a sit-down game and a good one to follow active singing. Children sit in a circle. Children must name flowers which are shown by a mother or other party helper. Bring in one flower at a time. Suggestions include a sunflower, rose, daffodil, violet, tulip, carnation, and iris. Artificial flowers may be used if real ones are not available.

Refreshments

Chicken loaf*
Spiced peach on endive leaf
Hot biscuits
Butter   Grape jelly
Milk
(Coffee for mothers)
Rhubarb pie   or   Lime sherbet

Devotions

In the book of Proverbs is a marvelous tribute of a young king to his mother. The chapter is long and not all of it is appropriate for the children. However, a minimum of a dozen verses from this chapter could be used effectively in closing devotions for this Mother's Day party. Ask two of the mothers to follow the reading of the Scripture with prayers.

* See Party Recipes section in back of book.

FLAG PARTY

Although a flag party is not traditional, it may be different enough to be highly interesting and challenging to primary age children. This party will be educational basically, but also fun.

Decorations

Use a large map of the United States to decorate the wall. Place American Christian flags at either side of the map. These flags are probably available in the church. Cover the refreshment table with red, white, and blue crepe paper runners. Uncle Sam's patriotic top hat would make a good centerpiece.

Things to Do

(1) *Puzzle of U.S.A.* There are several excellent jig-saw puzzles of the United States. Some of these are as large as four feet across. But regardless of size, one of these puzzles should be very challenging to primary children.

(2) *Stunts and songs.* Your local library will have resources for both stunts and songs concerning the flag.

(3) *Christian flag.* Ask your Sunday school superintendent to tell the story of the origin of the Christian flag.

(4) *Patriotic ceremony.* The following patriotic ceremony may be used effectively in this party:

1. Pledge of allegiance to the American flag.
2. Sing "My Country 'Tis of Thee."
3. Pledge of allegiance to the Christian flag.
4. Sing "Onward Christian Soldiers."

(5) *Records of patriotic songs.* Both the secular and religious record companies will have an ample supply of patriotic songs appropriate for primary children.

(6) *March time.* No patriotic flag party would be complete without a grand march. If possible get a record of John Philip Sousa's stirring "Stars and Stripes Forever."

(7) *Other flags.* Flags of other nations may be used to give an international flavor to the party. Something about the nation, the people, and the flag should be told when it is shown. Party helpers who have been assigned this project in advance can get ample information from the children's encyclopedias.

(8) *Seven league boots.* This is a relay race with the runners wearing large paper bags over their feet. Each runner must take off the sacks from around his own feet and give them to the next person after he

has finished his lap. A person who kicks a hole in the sack becomes disqualified.

Refreshments

Use vanilla ice cream for a patriotic sundae. Place fresh or frozen blueberries on one side and fresh or frozen strawberries on the other. Serve with sugar cookies and lemonade.

Devotions

Although boys and girls are somewhat aware of the cost involved in establishing the American flag, few of them have much idea of the cost involved in establishing the Christian flag. As an illustration of this cost, tell the boys and girls the story of Paul and Silas in the Philippian jail. Close with the song, "Must Jesus Bear the Cross Alone?"

IV. Party Ideas for Juniors

A PASTOR'S PARTY

It may be good on occasion for the boys and girls in the church to honor their pastor with a party. It will serve to impress them with his leadership in the congregation and may give both him and them an opportunity to get better acquainted. This is especially appropriate if the minister is new to the church.

Decorations

The room may be decorated for this occasion by placing two chairs in a central place for the minister and his wife. A large pulpit Bible and a candelabra may be placed on a table near the minister.

Things to Do

(1) *Name tags*. Be sure everyone has a name tag which will help to identify him to the minister and his wife.

(2) *Introductions*. Use your imagination in finding as many ways to introduce children as possible. Introduce the youngest child, the oldest child, etc. For the introductions nearly every child can have some distinguishing characteristic.

(3) *Program*. Plan a nice program to present to the minister and his wife, using as many children as possible. Readings, welcome speeches, prayers, and musical numbers may be used.

(4) *Hymns*. Sing one or more hymns which refer to the shepherd. Not only was Christ known as the Good Shepherd, but also the minister is the shepherd of his earthly flock.

(5) *Bible reading*. Several passages which are suitable for reading at a Pastor's Party include the following:

    Ephesians 4:4-7
    Ephesians 4:11-13
    John 21:15-17
    I Peter 5:1-4

Refreshments

    Decorated cupcakes
    Dixie ice cream cups
        Punch

Devotions

For devotions ask the pastor to conclude the party with appropriate remarks. It may be suggested that he use one of several references Jesus made to children.

LINCOLN'S BIRTHDAY SUPPER

Lincoln's Birthday Supper may be planned to precede another evening activity such as a church service, school play, or sports event. Since the children are aware of Lincoln through their regular school studies, it will be good for the church group to sponsor a party around this theme.

Decorations

Make a log cabin of cardboard for a centerpiece. Decorate paper napkins with the date February 12th. Construct a small rail fence down the middle of the table. Some children may have a "Lincoln Log" set which can be used for building a wonderful centerpiece.

Things to Do

(1) *Musical chairs.* While the meal is being prepared the children may enjoy playing one or two games. As the music is played either on the piano or record player, the children march around the chairs. There is always one less chair than children. When the music stops, there is a wild scramble for a chair. The game reaches a climax when the chairs are reduced to one and the players to two. The game may be played with cushions in a line on the floor.

(2) *Who is thy neighbor?* The children are divided into two teams. One team is blindfolded and seated in alternate chairs in a circle. The other team is seated quietly in the vacant chairs. At a signal from their captain, they all sing together a song chosen when they were out of the room. Now it is up to each member of the blindfolded team to identify his singing neighbor to the right or left. It is up to the first team to disguise their voices in whatever manner seems appropriate. If any neighbors have not been identified after the song is finished it may be repeated.

(3) *Records.* If any more time is needed before the meal is prepared, favorite gospel records may be played for the group.

Refreshments

Meat loaf
Scalloped potatoes
Whole kernel corn
Carrot and celery sticks
Sweet pickles
Milk
Warm gingerbread
Whipped cream

Devotions

Even the enemies of Abraham Lincoln called him, "Honest Abe." This dinner may be a good time to emphasize the lesson of honesty. For devotions, read the Ten Commandments and then make application to the one on honesty. The honest and dishonest man are like the brothers in the closing paragraph of the Sermon on the Mount who built their houses, one on the sand and the other on the rock. This parable may be told to illustrate the difference between a life built on honesty and sincerity over against a life built on hypocrisy and dishonesty.

JUNIOR CHRISTMAS PARTY

Although Juniors have learned to distinguish the difference between fairy tales and Bible stories, they are just beginning to distinguish well between the Santa Claus side of Christmas and the story of the manger. Any Christmas party planned for juniors should have a strong spiritual emphasis.

Decorations

If possible, decorate the party room with a manger scene. Japanese imports and American plastics have reduced the costs of these replicas. Any other decorations should be of the home type such as a Christmas tree. However, all Santa Claus references should be excluded.

Things to Do

(1) *Christmas package.* Present one large package to the guests. As music is played, have your guests hand it from person to person around the circle. As soon as the music stops, the one holding the package tells his name and takes off one of the wrappings. The idea is to wrap the package many times so that it will need to be unwrapped a dozen or more times until the gift is reached. The gift may be some simple thing such as a Christmas candy cane or small toy. The person removing the last wrapping receives the small gift.

(2) *Christmas card.* Give everyone a large Christmas card and then allow participants time to secure autographs and favorite Scripture references from all the people at the party. Suggest to them that this card be kept for years to come as a reminder of the party.

(3) *Christmas candles.* On a table, line up a dozen lighted candles. Ask the children to compete among themselves to see who can blow out the most candles in one breath. Give a decorated candle as a prize to the winner.

(4) *Christmas records.* There are many beautiful Christmas records available from both secular and Christian suppliers. These may be used for twenty minutes or more of wonderful entertainment for the children. Use only records with a sacred theme.

(5) *Gift exchange.* No party with juniors would be complete unless there was opportunity for a gift exchange.

Refreshments

Potato chips with dips
Christmas cookies
Ice cream balls
Hot chocolate with marshmallows

Devotions

Read the first twenty-one verses from the second chapter of the Gospel of St. Luke. After emphasizing the true meaning of Christmas ask for several individual prayers by the children. Close the devotions with the entire group reciting the Lord's Prayer.

OUTER SPACE PARTY

In this day and age when children are exceedingly conscious of space travel, the idea of an Outer Space Party may really catch on. Some of the children may have space suits for play. Adult sponsors may add an extra dimension of intrigue to the party by wearing their own version of space apparel, perhaps gold or silver with space emblems sewn on the shoulders.

Decorations

Space hats for everyone may be made from blue or gold tissue paper fastened to the head with cellophane tape. They may be trimmed with gold stars and yellow fringe. Yellow and blue balloons may also be used for outer space decorations. A table cloth may be made of blue crepe paper decorated with stars cut from gold foil wrapping paper and scattered at random over the cloth.

Things to Do

(1) *Flying saucer contest*. Make flying saucers out of aluminum foil pie pans fastened together. Each player may be given his turn for three attempts at throwing the flying saucer through a circle made of wire.

(2) *Film*. Many public libraries have cartoon type films explaining travel in outer space.

(3) *Ice holding contest*. An endurance trial with ice may be quite amusing. The contestants sit in a row of chairs each holding a large cake of ice in his hands. The person who holds the ice longest is the winner.

(4) *Predicament and solution*. After all the guests are seated in a circle, ask each person to whisper a predicament to the person on his left and a solution to the person on his right. For instance, the predicament might be, "What would you do if you were late for church Sunday morning?" A solution might be, "I would pull my hat down over my eyes." After everyone has been given both a predicament and a solution, the leader comes out with his predicament addressing the question to anyone on the opposite side of the circle. That player answers with the solution that was given to him and in turn gives his predicament to another player. The mixed up questions and answers are always fun.

(5) *Bubble gum contest*. Each contestant is given two sticks of bubble gum and allowed time to chew it properly. At a given signal each person endeavors to blow a large bubble. The person with the largest bubble wins.

(6) *Marble dash teaspoon relay*. An interesting relay race may be staged by having the teams carry two marbles in a teaspoon over a given route.

(7) *The "no" stunt.* The sponsor challenges the children by saying she can make them say, "No" if she wants them to. Since everyone knows a considerable amount of conversation can be carried on without the use of the word "no," there probably will be several persons to accept the challenge. The sponsor lines up these challengers in front of her and looks at them with a big question mark on her face. Suddenly she blurts out, "Oh, you know this trick anyhow, don't you?" It is likely that several in the group will blurt out a fast, "No."

(8) *Visit a planetarium.* In some cities plans may be made for the group to visit a planetarium where a good lecture on outer space can be both entertaining and educational.

Refreshments

Flying saucer burgers
Star-shaped molded salad
Potato chips
Star and crescent shaped cookies
Ice cream planet balls
Chocolate milk

Devotions

The story of Elijah riding to heaven on a chariot of fire should be an intriguing basis for closing devotions after an Outer Space Party.

GROWN-UP PARTY

Ask the children to come dressed in the costumes which represent a vocation or profession they feel they might like to follow when they are grown up. The children may want to come as cowboys, engineers, firemen, doctors, school teachers, businessmen, or preachers. Offer a prize for the best costume. A spiritual theme may be worked into the party by emphasizing the need for seeking God's will early in life as to vocational choice.

Decorations

The refreshment table may contain a centerpiece made of miniature dolls representing several professions such as a nurse, doctor, railroad man, etc. Miniature equipment for various occupations may also be used: hammers, thermometers, needle and thread.

Things to Do

(1) *Know your Bible professions.* A very challenging paper and pencil game may be made on Bible professions. This must be geared to the knowledge of the children. Some starting suggestions are as follows:

Peter—fisherman
Jesus—carpenter
Paul—tentmaker
Moses—shepherd
David—musician
Zaccheus—tax collector
Luke—doctor
Joseph—carpenter
Lydia—dealer in purple
Abraham—rancher
Demetrius—gold and silver smith
Amos—herdsman

(2) *Tell time.* Give each child an opportunity to tell why he has chosen the particular occupation he represents.

(3) *Bible flash cards.* Construct a set of flash cards with names of Bible characters and their vocations. Use only names and vocations which have been studied during the last months or year. Each child will pick a card from the stack and then will tell what he knows about the particular character and his vocation. After this child has told all he or she knows others from the group may want to add to the story.

(4) *Church house.* Each player is given the name of something which is a part of the church, such as steeple, pulpit, altar, window, stairs, front door, back door, water fountain, choir room, etc. The storyteller spins the yarn of a visit to the church on a Sunday morning. As the player tells the story, the parts mentioned get up and follow him as he marches about the room. When he yells, "Benediction," each player scrambles

96

for a seat. The one left out becomes the next storyteller.

(5) *Know your sounds.* The leader is hidden behind the screen with necessary props. The children are given paper and pencil on which to write their guesses for the noises which he hears. The person with the right electronic equipment may record the sounds and play them on a tape recorder for the party. The following list is suggested:
1. Sawing wood
2. Winding a clock
3. Eating celery
4. Counting silver change
5. Squeaking rubber dolls
6. Breaking a dish
7. Striking a match
8. Driving a nail
9. Sipping through a straw

(6) *Mind reading.* This game is suitable for children in the fourth grade or above. The leader chooses an accomplice and gives her the clue. She leaves the room and the group decides upon some object in the room. She returns and the leader starts asking, "Is it the lamp?" "Is it the table?" etc. The accomplice says, "No," until the leader names the object decided upon. The clue is that the right object always will be the first thing named after something black in color.

Refreshments

       Tuna salad in
       Hot dog buns
Pickles   Cheese cubes
      Jello dessert

Devotions

Ask each child to pray aloud for someone who is in the vocation they represent. Telling about a soldier's armament described by Paul* may also be used for closing devotions.

* Ephesians 6.

UNITED NATIONS PARTY

United Nations was established in 1945 on April 25th as the "United Nations Conference on National Organizations" when it met in session in San Francisco at the flag-bedecked War Memorial building. This theme may be used for a fall party for boys and girls. With only a slight adjustment it can well be made into a missionary theme.

Decorations

If possible, decorate the room with the flags of many nations. Often these can be secured from travel agencies, public organizations, or even from variety stores. A cake decorated with the American flag may be used as a centerpiece for the refreshment table.

Things to Do

(1) *Costumes with a purpose.* Ask each guest to come dressed in a costume which illustrates some religious activity such as a native missionary garb, famous Christians, Puritan, or others. Or, the children may be asked to come dressed in the garb of a foreign country. Award a prize to the child with the most accurate, unique, and original idea in his costume.

(2) *Missionary Christmas.* Collect gifts for missionaries overseas and assemble them at the party to be mailed prior to November 1st. If it seems appropriate, a small lighted Christmas tree may be used as a focal point for gathering the presents. While the children are at the party they may be asked to write letters to the missionaries, to be sent with their packages.

(3) *Kangaroo race.* A rubber balloon inflated to about six inches in diameter must be held between the knees in this novelty race. While racing, either by hopping or shuffling along, the contestants are required to keep hands on hips. An appropriate distance for the race is about sixty feet. If a player breaks his balloon, he is disqualified. If he loses it but it is still inflated, he can pick it up, run back to the starting line and begin again. This race may be run either forward or backward. Bean bags may be used instead of balloons.

(4) *Igloo eating contest.* To represent the countries of the frozen north, the children may enter into an igloo eating contest. White mound-shaped cookies which can be bought in most grocery stores may be used to represent the igloos. It may be a challenge among the boys to see who can eat the most.

(5) *African safari.* While someone has been sent from the room, the group decides on a particular object which represents the lion in

the African safari. When the child returns to the room the group will clap loudly when the child is close to the object and more softly as the child moves away from it. By the sound of the clapping the child can finally be led to guess the imaginary lion.

(6) *English kick ball.* If the party is held in a large area or if the weather permits an outdoor activity, organize the children into a circle with half of them inside it. A kick ball is thrown by a child in the outer circle. He tries to hit some one on the inside of the ring. As a child is hit he joins the circle and becomes a part of the group who throws the ball toward those who are left inside. The last child left inside the circle is winner.

Refreshments
    Hot dogs
    Popsicles
    Brownies

Devotions

If possible, arrange to have the Lord's Prayer said in several different languages. If there are no persons available to speak in a foreign language, perhaps a suitable closing devotion can be made by reading the first paragraph of the second chapter of Acts which enumerates all of the various countries represented in Jerusalem on the day of Pentecost. Ask several children to participate in prayers for peoples of other nations.

PARTY FOR A SICK CHILD

This is not a party in the regular sense of the word. However, there are occasions among many groups of children when someone needs to be honored and possibly entertained by a group of children in the church. Boys and girls who suffer from leg injuries or other problems of this sort are often involved in a long convalescence which does not keep them from enjoying the company of children who may come to entertain them.

Decorations

Portable decorations may be used to brighten up the sick room. Colorful balloons and streamers are probably the most easily used for this purpose.

Things to Do

(1) *Bulletin board or screen.* This may be provided in the room for privacy. The children may bring picture cards or messages which can be pinned onto the board and read by the child after the party is over.

(2) *Fish bowl.* Place a fish bowl within sight of the bed. One or two fish may be provided for the beginning of an intriguing hobby which the child may follow during the period of the long convalescence.

(3) *Bird food.* Hang a soap-strainer filled with a paste or pudding of suet, peanut butter, and bird seed on a branch or in a receptacle just outside the window of the sick room. As the birds fly to the food the child may be greatly entertained and even come to develop a keen appreciation for his feathered friends.

(4) *Dish garden.* A small garden may be started for the sick child by planting carrots or sweet potatoes in a box. Place the box near the window. The growing process of the vegetable will probably be intriguing to the child.

(5) *Scrap book.* Supply the child with a large scrap book which can be used for keeping cards and letters which he accumulates during the time of his illness.

(6) *Carving.* Clay or soap may be presented to the child for carving.

(7) *Writing case.* An excellent gift is a writing case containing paper, envelopes, and pencils. The name of the child may be printed on the stationery, on the envelopes, and even on the pencils.

(8) *Games.* For a sick child some of the games which may be especially appropriate include the following: checkers, chess, chinese checkers, dominoes, anagrams, parchesi, puzzles, and riddles. Also educational flash cards will be useful.

Refreshments

The kind of refreshments which may be served for a sick child depend almost entirely on the condition of the child and on circumstances. Check with the nurse or parent in charge. A good thing to keep in mind is that jello can be set in paper cups. This serves as the individual dish and can be eaten with plastic spoons.

Devotions

Ask each child to bring his own Testament to the party. At devotions time instruct the children to open their Testaments to the Beatitudes in the fifth chapter of Matthew. Let the children take turns, each reading one of the Beatitudes. They may close by all reading together the Lord's Prayer in the next chapter.

ACTIVITY PARTY

Oftentimes it is good for juniors to become involved in some special activity rather than to have a party in the traditional sense. There are many places children can go and many things they can do which will not only entertain them but oftentimes be of real educational value. After the excursion has been finished it may be well to bring the children to the church or a private home for refreshments and devotions.

Decorations

The decorations will depend almost entirely on the activity planned for this party. In any case, the decorations may be very simple.

Things to Do

1. Visit a zoo.
2. Play garden golf.
3. Go to an archery gallery.
4. Go bowling.
5. Take a boat trip.
6. Visit a museum.
7. Visit a factory.
8. Visit a bakery.
9. Visit a college.
10. Visit another church.
11. Go swimming.
12. Take a hike.
13. Go to an amusement park.
14. Attend a sports event.
15. Visit a bank.
16. Visit an airport.
17. Visit the State Capitol.
18. Visit the newspaper office.
19. Visit a cannery.
20. Visit a restaurant kitchen.
21. Attend a concert.
22. Attend a revival service.
23. Visit a dairy.
24. Visit a farm or ranch.

Refreshments

Chili
Crackers
Milk
Ice cream eskimo pies

Devotions

The thirteenth chapter of St. Matthew contains a list of parables Jesus told. Use any one or group of these as a basis for closing devotions.

JUNGLE VILLAGE PARTY

The plans for this party require a wooded area of sufficient foliage to isolate the group for the evening. After meeting at a designated spot, the children will be taken on a hike through the "jungle" to the place where they will have the party.

Decorations

As nearly as possible, arrange the party area to look like a native village. Build a campfire in front of a lean-to shack. A second or third campfire may be built to give both light and warmth. If possible, arrange for a large black pot to be placed over one of the campfires. Atmosphere may be further created with the use of tom-tom drums.

Things to Do

(1) *Songs.* No songs are more wonderful than those sung out-of-doors around an open fire. Plan these in advance. Someone in the group may be able to play an accordion, guitar, or other portable instrument.

(2) *Story time.* Two or three good missionary stories may be told to the group as they sit about the fire. These stories should be top quality, filled with suspense, and well done. Your pastor or even the supplier in your local Christian book store can be of help in securing the right stories.

(3) *Testimonies.* Arrange in advance to have fairly large chips of wood dipped into a flammable material and stacked at a safe distance from the fire. As each person gives his testimony he throws a chip of wood onto the fire to make an immediate increase in the blaze.

(4) *Centipede race.* Line up the boys in groups of four, five or six. Each group straddles a pole. Cane fishing poles are particularly good for this purpose. Each boy grips the pole in front of him with one hand and behind him with the other. It is necessary for the legs on one side of the pole to move in unison or hopeless confusion results.

Refreshments

Roast weiners over the fire. Have a large thermos of Kool-aid or a cooler filled with bottled pop. Marshmallows toasted on the coals may be eaten with cookies.

Devotions

Several alternatives will work well for closing devotions in a party of this nature. A story may be told with sound effects. Or some person dressed in a native garb may tell a missionary story in the first person. Or the story of the shipwreck of Paul on the island of Malta as recorded in the book of Acts may be read and used as a basis for comment. Several prayers may be used in conclusion.

A WELCOME PARTY

A Welcome Party may be given to all the children who have been promoted from the primary department into the junior department. Or a welcome theme may be appropriate when a number of children have joined the department.

Decorations

Your own imagination must be used in devising means for decorations on the theme of welcome. Signs on the wall, party hats, welcome badges, and other means may be used to promote the idea of welcome. The cake may be decorated with the word "welcome" in the center of it. Styrofoam may be used for cutting out the letters WELCOME which can then be colored or decorated with flowers and sequins.

Things to Do

(1) *Introductions.* Introduce all of the teachers in the new department. Take time to allow the children to understand who they are and what their background is. Also take time for the children to be introduced to all the teachers.

(2) *Pictures.* If possible arrange to have pictures exchanged between the children and the teachers. Almost all children enjoy having a picture of their teacher. The pictures of the children will help teachers to associate faces with names.

(3) *Treasure hunt, hot and cold.* Wrap small prizes and hide them in various parts of the room. The leader should be familiar with the hiding places of each package. As a child walks slowly to various parts of the room he can turn to the leader who will say either "Hot" or "Cold" to help him find a prize.

(4) *Funny faces. It* is in the center of the circle of children and tries to make the others laugh by making funny faces, sticking out his tongue, wiggling his ears, staring at the players, making idiotic sounds, dancing, singing, or poking fun at the players. As the players laugh or smile, they join those inside the circle and attempt to make the remaining ones laugh. The game ends when only one person is left outside the circle.

(5) *Cracker swat.* Two boys are blindfolded and asked to kneel on the floor just far enough apart so that they can barely reach each other. A cracker is laid on top of each boy's head and both boys are given a rolled newspaper. Each boy must not only keep his cracker balanced on his head but try to break the other boy's cracker. The winner takes on the next competitor.

(6) *Clothespin drop.* Empty milk bottles and a bag of wooden clothespins are needed for this en-

tertaining game of skill. Divide the guests into two teams. Have teams stand in line facing each other with ample space between the rows. Each player in turn stands over the milk bottle and attempts at the signal to drop his clothespins one at a time into the bottle from the height of his nose. The team which succeeds in bottling the greatest number of clothespins wins.

(7) *Musical shoe.* This is a variation of musical chairs. Instead of the children moving, the shoe goes from hand to hand around the circle of children seated on the floor. The child who holds it when the music stops has to leave the circle. For a variation the shoe may be passed from hand to hand behind the children's backs.

(8) *Dogs and cats.* Hide wrapped candies over the entire area to be used for the party. Appoint one person on each side as the captain of the "cats" and the "dogs." When each captain has chosen a team and the signal is given, the "dogs" and "cats" go out to try to find their loot. When they find a wrapped candy they are to bark like a dog or meow like a cat until their captain comes to pick up the candy. The captains will be very busy scurrying about from place to place. The team with the most candies at the end of the given period of time wins.

Refreshments

Have a large sheet cake decorated with the word "Welcome." Ask someone to cut and serve the cake as the children pass the refreshment table carrying their own plate. A punch bowl at the end of the table will serve as a festive decoration for the party.

Devotions

Use all of the new children in the closing devotions. Give each of these children an opportunity to draw a 3 x 5 card from a hat or other receptacle. On the card will be a verse of Scripture. As the new children stand in a line with their cards, ask an older member of the group to come and stand by each child. After the new child has read his verse of Scripture, the older child will make a short prayer of thanks for this new member of the group. The closing prayer may be made by the supervisor.

JUNIOR HALLOWE'EN PARTY

Although Juniors are much more sophisticated than the primary children, it is still important to plan a junior party which will not be too frightening. Almost any place is good for a junior Hallowe'en party. A barn, shed, garage, basement room, or fellowship hall are all suitable places.

Decorations

A hollowed-out pumpkin filled with shiny red apples, grapes, and nuts, is simple but attractive for the table. Apples may be hollowed out for candle holders. A row of these "apple candles" placed on the mantle makes a pretty setting.

A plump, smiling pumpkin on a scalloped circle of green crepe paper surrounded by a bevy of grinning apples makes a cheerful centerpiece. With a sharp knife, cut out eyes, noses, and grinning mouths in each apple and in the pumpkin. Dress apples in peaked hats made by slitting doilies to the center and overlapping the edges. Make pumpkin hat of black construction paper. Secure the hats with toothpicks or corsage pins. Place apples around the pumpkin.

Things to Do

(1) *The witch whistle.* A circle is formed with everyone facing in. *It* stands in the circle and points to a child and tells him what to do, performing the action himself. Each time he says, "Witch, nod your head," or "Witch, smile," the rest of the players must do the same. Suddenly he points to a player saying, "Witch, whistle!" If the startled guest fails to whistle before *It* counts to ten, the child becomes the new *It*.

(2) *Witch's cat.* When properly dissected, any witch's cat is found to contain the following astonishing things:

1. A kind of tree (Fir)
2. A silent delay (pause)
3. A group of words making complete sense (clause)
4. A story (tale)
5. What mice do when they hear the cat (hide)
6. Often heard in the talk of an egotist (I)
7. Burma Shave made a fortune off them (whiskers)
8. A comb has these (teeth)
9. A unit of measure (feet)
10. They grow on cornstalks (ears)

(3) *Ghost walk.* Plan to blindfold the children and have them walk the "ghost walk." Have an electric fan blowing to make them feel a blast of cold air, and an electric heater for a blast of hot air. Set up a hole to peek through where they see a scary scene. Be sure to plan

many other strange sensations and sounds as they make their way along the ghost walk.

(4) *Passing of Mr. Smith.* One person reads the poem and another person passes around the proper objects. This is most fun when all the lights are out while Mr. Smith's remains are passed.

The truth it is, and not a myth,
That once there lived a man named Smith;
And it came his mournful lot,
To be murdered quite near this spot.

We now will pass out his remains.
You first will handle poor Smith's BRAINS.
(pass moist sponges around the group)

The head once crowned with locks so fair,
Lies low; here comes Smith's nice soft HAIR.
(pass corn silk or fur)

Sweet music Smith once loved to hear,
It fell upon his gentle EAR.
(pass dried peaches for ears)

When Smith would smile at boys and girls,
His TEETH gleamed out like whitest pearls.
(pass dried kernels of corn)

And now the next you'll scarce hold true,
We pass his WINDPIPE out to you.
(pass links of uncut cold cooked macaroni)

* See Party Recipes section in back of book.

The next you soon will understand,
Is simply poor old Smith's right HAND.
(pass kid glove filled with wet sand)

Smith's vision once was keen and wise,
You'll know it when you touch his EYES.
(pass skinned grapes)

(5) *Miscellaneous.* Bobbing for apples, treasure hunt, dart-throwing contest, dropping clothespins into a small hollowed-out pumpkin, and a balloon breaking contest are all fun for this season.

(6) *Reverse trick or treat.* The children may go in a group to visit several homes of elderly people where they can leave small gifts.

Refreshments

Fill hot dog buns with tuna salad and wrap in aluminum foil, twisting the ends. These may be heated over an open fire or in a fireplace. Have someone in a witch's costume presiding over a large kettle of hot spiced apple cider.* Serve the "brew" with an old-fashioned dipper.

Devotions

Close the party by singing several choruses the children love. Read the 150th Psalm on making a joyful noise unto the Lord. Ask one of the older junior children to conclude the party with prayer.

A JIFFY PARTY

Many mothers are just too busy to spend much time in preparing a party ahead of time; this party is designed to help plan an entertainment which can be organized quickly and with a minimum of effort.

Decorations

After you have telephoned the invitations, make a quick trip to the variety store where you may buy at little expense a good supply of snappers and balloons. While waiting for the guests to arrive, inflate the balloons and heap them in the center of the table. Tie ribbons from the balloons to favors for the children. Lollipops may be used as favors. Use chewing gum, candy bars, or comic books for game prizes. To shorten shopping time, buy only gifts which are suitable for both boys and girls, such as crayons, soap bubble sets, or comics. If shopping time is impossible, give each child a shiny dime scotch-taped to a card.

Things to Do

(1) *Name the States*. Have a contest to name the fifty States; and then name the capitols.

(2) *A paper bag relay race*. Give each child a paper bag. He runs to the end of the course where he inflates his bag and breaks it. Then he runs back to the foot of the line for the next person to begin his part of the race.

(3) *Bubble gum blowing contest*. Supply bubble gum. Children will do their own contest.

(4) *Play Monoply*.

(5) *Play Anagrams*.

(6) *Use a 16mm colored film* of a travelogue or children's story.

(7) *A bean race*. Divide the children into two groups. Allowing them to carry but one bean at a time, see which team can be first to transport a pile of beans from one location to another.

(8) *Artist's contest*. Give each child paper and crayons and allow them ten minutes for producing the finest picture they can of some scene through the nearby window or an object on a table in the room.

(9) *Musical chairs*.

(10) *Limerick contest*. Give the children the first part of a limerick and see who can come up with the best final line. Here is a suggestion:

Our church has served us well these years,
We love the people 'most to tears,
But this one thing we do not like
....

(11) *Famous slogans*. Give the children a stack of magazines and let them devise their own contest with

each other identifying products by slogans.

Refreshments

Serve ice cream log roll or dixie cups for dessert. The dairy will deliver an ample supply of orange drink to your back door.

Devotions

From a modern language version of the New Testament, read the story in the fifteenth chapter of Luke of the lost sheep. Plan for an adult or older child to sing "The Ninety and Nine." Close with prayer.

NORTH POLE PARTY

There is a lot of fun to be had in the winter time for people who enjoy the out-of-doors. Oftentimes a combination of outdoor activity and inside refreshments can make for a wonderful day or evening.

Decorations

No decorations are really needed for a North Pole party. However, paper Eskimos, totem poles, artificial snow, and miniature dog sleds may be used to advantage. If possible, plan for a roaring fire in the fireplace. If a fireplace is not possible, perhaps an artificial fire can be made in the room.

Things to Do

(1) *Sledding.*

(2) *Sleigh ride.*

(3) *Shovel walks* for an elderly couple.

(4) *Build a snowman.*

(5) *Make snow ice cream.* Mix a quantity of clean snow with milk, sugar, and vanilla flavoring.

(6) *Make popcorn.*

(7) *Favorite records.* Ask each one to bring his favorite record which may be played while the group is sitting about relaxing following the outdoor activity.

Refreshments

Toasted cheese sandwiches
Sweet pickles
Hot chocolate

Devotions

A man in the Old Testament named Benaiah is famous because he "slew a lion in a pit on a snowy day" (I Chronicles 11:22).

The following applications may be made to this story: 1) Every person faces his share of lions in life. The lions consist of the challenges with which we cope day after day. If we think it is unfair for us to face big lions while others are unchallenged, we are only mistaken. Everyone has his share.

2) Benaiah slew the lion in the lion's own territory. If the pit was the home of the lion, or if the lion had been trapped there, it really makes no difference. The facts are that Benaiah had a great disadvantage in facing this particular challenge in his life.

3) Benaiah slew the lion on a snowy day. Snow on the ground meant that Benaiah had a very difficult time in fighting his battle. But the person who meets the challenges of life under the most difficult circumstances and still is a victor and not a victim, is the person who gets the greatest joy from living.

HOBO PARTY

Children of junior age enjoy dressing up to imitate special groups among the adults such as firemen, cowboys, and policemen. One of these strange groups which children always enjoy emulating is the hoboes. A party built around the hobo theme is always popular.

Decorations

Make this a basement party with rags in the windows and patches tacked on the curtains. Candles placed in tin cans and bottles help to add to the atmosphere. Lunch may be served in bandana knapsacks tied to a stick. Signs about the room should read, "Beware of dog," "No tramps allowed," "Keep out!" These are the typical signs hoboes are accustomed to seeing.

Things to Do

(1) *Jerusalem and Jericho.* The leader stands where all can see him. The children are asked to stand in a line. The leader calls either Jerusalem or Jericho. If he says Jerusalem they all bow deeply, if he says Jericho no one moves. The leader attempts to confuse the group by acting opposite to what he says. Anyone bowing when he should not or failing to bow when he should must exchange places with the leader.

(2) *Balloon volleyball.* Stretch a piece of ordinary string between two posts in the basement or between the backs of two chairs. The rubber balloon must be batted over the string which serves in the place of a volleyball net. The team which allows the balloon to touch the floor on its side of string gives one point to the opposite team. The winning score is fifteen.

(3) *Potato race.* The children are divided into partners for this race. Each pair chooses to be a different animal, such as dog, rooster, cow, donkey, or cat. Twenty or thirty potatoes are scattered about the floor. One of the partners of each pair is blindfolded. At the signal the race begins. The blindfolded member of each team must pick up the potatoes one at a time and take them back to his partner who guides him by making the sound of the animal they have chosen. Players must listen only to the he-haws, moo-moos, crowing, or barks of their partner to search successfully for the potatoes. The sound indicates whether the blindfolded person is hot or cold in regard to the potatoes. The pair who gathers the most potatoes is the winner.

(4) *Sculpture contest.* Provide newspapers to work on. Have an assortment of paring knives and large bars of soap, potatoes, and modeling clay. Have a sculpture exhibit and offer a prize for the best work.

(5) *Film.* Several 16mm films using either live characters or cartoon figures feature the hobo. One of

these may be used with great success for this party.

Refreshments

Baked beans in covered paper cup
(serve with plastic spoon)
Chicken drumstick wrapped in foil
Buttered roll
Bottled soda pop

Devotions

Read or tell the story of the twelve spies who were sent by Moses into the Promised Land. Indicate that the wanderings of the children of Israel for forty years were made because of their lack in courage and faith toward a national goal. Close with several prayers by the children.

FATHER'S DAY PARTY

This need not be a fancy affair. Make arrangements for the fathers and sons to be involved in some special activity such as: playing baseball in the park, going on a fishing expedition, taking a boat ride, going to a hockey game or attending a sports event. A get-together in the church recreation rooms for ping pong and other such activities may also be appreciated. Plain food is the best food for fathers and sons. Sandwiches should be generously filled. Ice cream should have good topping. If the Father's Day party is to follow the traditional pattern instead of an excursion, then a large room where noise won't bother will be the best place for the group.

Decorations

Decorate with sports equipment such as old golf clubs, baseball bats, hockey sticks, and tennis rackets.

Things to Do

(1) *Simon says*. Players stand about with plenty of room between each player for action. The leader calls a command such as, "Simon says, hands on hips and bend body." As Simon calls out each of the commands on what the person should do everyone obeys explicitly. However, if the command is not preceded by "Simon says" the players do nothing. Any player failing to obey immediately a "Simon says" command or any obeying a command not prefaced by "Simon says" must drop out. The leader makes it more confusing by going through the actions each time himself.

(2) *Chef boxing*. Six to a dozen men or more can play this game. An area suitable to the number of players should be roped off. Each contestant wears a paper bag hat making him resemble a chef. Furnish each player with a rolled up newspaper. This is a battle royal. At the starting signal, every player tries to knock off some other player's hat. When a player's hat is knocked off he must leave the ring immediately. The winner of the battle is the man who keeps his hat on the longest. This is no game for sissies. Chef boxing can become really rough. However, it is a wonderful spectator game. The game may be varied by asking each of the fathers to carry a boy on his back. It is the boys then who wield the paper rolls.

(3) *Dad and lad dinner*. On some occasions it may be best to plan a dinner instead of a party. If so, a suggested order of program is listed below:

1. Invocation
2. Welcome speech
3. Group singing
4. Introductions
5. Prizes

6. Reading
7. Group singing
8. Dinner
9. Musical program
10. Talk by a father
11. Talk by a son
12. Closing devotions

Refreshments

Ham sandwiches
Potato chips
Ice cream with fresh
or
Frozen strawberries
Coffee   Cold drinks

Devotions

If possible, secure a library copy of the Edgar A. Guest poem, "The Too Busy Father." A father and son may take alternate verses as they read the 13th chapter of I Corinthians. Another father and son combination may be asked to conclude the party with prayers.

FALL ROUND-UP PARTY

This can be a party with a purpose. In the Fall of the year, just after school has opened, all the boys and girls may be invited to a Saturday afternoon party at the church as a special Sunday school promotion rally. Invitations should be written on folded note paper in tan or beige. The more children the better.

Decorations

Ask each child to dress in a western costume, either cowboy or Indian. Each child will be asked to bring his own blanket for seating. No chairs will be used in the room. Provide a portable fence at the door over which each child must climb. If the room is large enough, a big tepee may be constructed in the center of the area.

Things to Do

(1) *Film.* Many travel films on the western areas may be used. Suggestions include visits to Yosemite, Grand Canyon, or a western ranch. Also, many wonderful religious films are available which will fit into the theme.

(2) *Program.* If there are scores of children present it may be much better to provide a program than games. Use as many boys and girls as possible on the program. Plan for an adult children's worker to lead them in both singing and worship.

(3) *Marching time.* If the children seem to become restless it may be well to get them on their feet in a march around the room.

(4) *Scripture verse roundup.* Ask several of the children to stand and give verses of Scripture which they can remember from their Sunday school work of the last year.

Refreshments

Chuck wagon stew, ranchers' biscuits, roundup ice cream (vanilla with nuts or dates in it), sunset cookies with orange frosting, pardner's drink (milk flavored with chocolate).

Devotions

Moses was in a ranching area when he saw the burning bush which would not be consumed. This story may be read or told to the children as a concluding devotion.

INDOOR PICNIC

In the dead of winter when outdoor picnics are difficult, if not impossible, the children may get great fun in having an indoor picnic. Active games will be planned. Picnic foods will be served. Children will dress in clothes suitable for active play.

Decorations

The best place for an indoor picnic is a large fellowship room or even a gymnasium. Ask each child to bring a blanket to sit on during games and refreshment time. A large sign across the end of the room with the words "Welcome to the picnic," will help create the party atmosphere.

Things to Do

(1) *Zip.* Players are asked to sit in a circle on their blankets. Each child gives special attention to his neighbor on the left. The leader in the center points to one of the children and says, "One, two, three, four, five, zip!" The person to whom he is pointing must shout the name of the person to his left before zip is called. If he fails to do this he must exchange places with the leader in the center. The game must move rapidly. If the crowd is large and the group active there may be several "zippers" in the center of the circle. When the leader shouts, "Boom — dash, zip!" all players must change seats. The children then must get acquainted rapidly with their new left hand neighbor for a "zipper" may be along any moment.

(2) *Feeding the elephant.* Place a megaphone so that it is slightly tilted with the mouthpiece down and the large end toward the line where the contestants will be standing. Have a basket or other receptacle beneath the megaphone to catch peanuts as they fall through. Each tosser is given ten peanuts. He tries to throw them one at a time into the elephant's mouth which is the large open end of the megaphone. The contestants should stand about eight to ten feet away from the mouth of the elephant. The person tossing the most peanuts into the "elephant's mouth" is the winner.

(3) *Discus throw.* Contestants are furnished with paper plates which they throw like a discus. The child who throws his the farthest is winner.

(4) *Pillowcase relay.* Line all of the children into two teams. Each team is provided with a bed pillow. At the signal the first child on each team takes the pillow out of the pillowcase and puts it back again. He then hands it to the next teammate who does the same thing. The first team to complete the operation is winner. Since each contestant is allowed to devise his own way for getting the pillow in the casing, some

will show greater skill than others because of their home chores.

(5) *Jump the creek*. The children form a single line. Two lines are drawn to represent the banks of the creek. The players run, one at a time, and try to jump the creek. If a player misses, he must drop out to get his feet dry. After each round, the creek is made a little wider. Thus, it may be determined who is the best creek-jumper.

(6) *Statue race*. If your party is being held in a very large room or gymnasium then the children will get lots of fun from a statue race. The leader stands between the starting line and the goal, facing the goal. The leader then counts aloud to ten, keeping his eyes covered or looking straight ahead. When he has called "ten" the leader uncovers his eyes and turns around. Immediately everyone must be perfectly still, holding whatever position they have at the time he finished counting to ten. If the leader discovers anyone moving, that player must go back to the starting position and begin over. The process continues until someone covers the course and is declared winner.

(7) *Weighing and measuring contest*. If the party consists of nearly an equal number of boys and girls, weigh and measure each child as they come to the picnic. The girls' or boys' side will enjoy winning with the most pounds in weight or the most inches in height.

(8) *Races*. There are any number of special kinds of races which can be handled indoors. These may be planned according to the size of the room.

Refreshments

Use paper plates and plastic spoons and forks. Serve potato salad, baked beans, hot dogs, potato chips, and your other favorite picnic foods. Serve lemonade to drink.

Devotions

Ask one of the children to read the first Psalm. If all of the children know the Psalm they may recite it together. Another outdoor Psalm which may be read by one of the children or recited by the group is the twenty-third Psalm. After two or three of these Psalms have been read, the children may enjoy some group singing before a closing prayer.

JUNIOR BIRTHDAY PARTY

The birthday parties celebrated by juniors are vitally important to them. It is happy recognition of their growing up. Also, junior children are closely attached to their friends. The occasion of a birthday party gives them opportunity to invite their friends to their home.

Decorations

The traditional decorated birthday cake and candles, balloons, colored crepe paper streamers, and party hats are sufficient decorations for a junior birthday party.

Things to Do

(1) *Ping pong ball bounce*. With the use of a string or rubber band, fasten three or four empty coffee cans together. Place these on the floor at a reasonable distance from the line where the contestants stand. The object of the game is to bounce the ping pong ball into one of the cans. Label each coffee can with a different score. The persons with the highest scores are winners.

(2) *Rattle and guess*. Secure a number of oatmeal boxes which have tops. Place different objects in each box and tape on the lid. Allow the children, in turn, to shake the containers and guess what is in each of them. Suggestions for things in the boxes may include keys, pennies, small potatoes, paper clips, marbles, and rubber erasers.

(3) *Blow and break*. Since junior boys and girls are especially proud of their maturity, involve them in a relay race which depends on each child's ability to blow up a balloon to the breaking point. Each child takes his own turn along the line in an attempt to blow up and break his balloon quickly. The side which finishes first is declared winner.

(4) *Obstacle race*. If the size of the room permits, plan an obstacle race for these junior boys and girls. Chairs, boxes, barrels, and even pieces of furniture may be used as obstacles in the race.

(5) *Birthday excursion*. An excursion to an amusement park, museum or other children's activity may be an excellent means for celebrating the birthday of a junior child. It sometimes can be a happy substitute for a more traditional birthday celebration.

Refreshments

    Birthday cake
    Ice cream
    Fruit punch

Devotions

The story of Jesus and His experience in Jerusalem when He was twelve years of age is an excellent

Scripture passage for closing devotions at a junior-age birthday party. Several lessons may be pointed out:

(1) Jesus at twelve years of age was beginning to bear considerable spiritual responsibility.

(2) Even though Jesus was unharmed, Mary and Joseph suffered considerably because He had been lost from them.

(3) Finding Jesus in the temple must indicate the importance of the church to our Saviour.

(4) Mary and Joseph needed Jesus as much as He needed them. Parents and children need each other.

V. Party Ideas for Junior High Young People

SUNRISE BREAKFAST

Many of the plans for this party will depend on where you live. In some parts of the country where it is warm almost four seasons a year, sunrise breakfasts are year-around favorites as parties for Junior High children. In other parts of the country, the idea simply needs to be introduced to become popular.

Build a fire, allow it to burn down to glowing embers. The food should be hearty with plenty for second and third helpings. Portable grills can be used to augment the open fire for cooking. The menu may consist of such things as whole oranges to be peeled, fried ham with eggs, plus cold-boiled potatoes sliced and fried.

Decorations

The only decorations needed for a party of this kind are checkered table cloths for all the tables and high chef's hats to be worn by the cooks. Gay aprons may also be used by the cooks and those who help serve.

Things to Do

(1) *Hike*. While the food is being cooked, the Junior Highers may be taken on a long walk around the lake, through the park, across the woods or wherever the path seems appropriate.

(2) *Bird watching*. If there is a practicing ornithologist in the church, let him direct the young folks in the art of watching for early morning birds. A small bird book is helpful in classifying and recognizing species.

(3) *Fox and geese*. If an active game seems appropriate, fox and geese should be suitable. Clear off paths on a level surface like the spokes in a wheel. The center where the paths cross is the goal. There may be more than one circle, one outside the other. The player who is the fox tries to tag one of the players who are the geese. If he succeeds, that player becomes the fox. No player must run out of the paths. Failure to observe this rule means that the offending player becomes the fox. The geese may jump across from one path to another but the fox cannot. Neither can the fox tag a goose across the paths. Any goose who occupies the center is safe. However, only one goose is safe at a time.

(4) *Laughing hat*. If a few more minutes are needed before the food is on the table this activity game may help prepare everyone for a bigger breakfast. Divide the group into two teams. Toss a hat into the air. If it lands with the top up, one side laughs immediately. If it lands bottom side up, the other side laughs. Any player who laughs at the wrong time drops out.

Refreshments

        Oranges
       Fried ham
Scrambled eggs   Fried potatoes
  Rolls   Butter
        Cocoa

Devotions

One of the most appropriate passages of Scripture for devotions at a sunrise breakfast is the passage which tells the story of Jesus and His disciples at the seaside breakfast in Galilee.

JUNIOR HIGH HALLOWE'EN PARTY

No age group appreciates a good old-fashioned Hallowe'en party more than the Junior High children. They still have vivid imaginations, are more sophisticated than the smaller children but far less adult than the Senior High young people. They enter enthusiastically into all kinds of games and contests. The Hallowe'en theme is a natural for them.

Decorations

Corn stalks, sheaves of wheat, pumpkins, apples, nuts, squash, red peppers, autumn leaves and branches, scarecrows, iron or brass kettles, reeds or grasses, crepe paper streamers, bats and witches, all make good decorations for Junior High parties. Select the ones that seem most appropriate to the party and arrange them around the rooms. Experimentation with different groupings and arrangements usually results in the best decorative effect.

Brooms or sticks dressed as ghosts, scarecrows, and skeletons may stand in dimly-lit corners or inside a dark closet. Cats and owls cut from construction paper can decorate windows, walls, or mirrors. Ask the Junior Highers to come in costume and thereby add life and decorations to the party.

A large thick yellow or orange candle reflected in a mirror makes an attractive mantel or table decoration. The table may be covered with a black sateen cloth. Crepe paper and a mirror surrounded with autumn leaves can be used in the center. The mantel mirror may be outlined in leaves or crepe paper festoons.

Things to Do

(1) *Apple-bob surprise.* Bobbing for apples is an old favorite for Hallowe'en parties and is always fun. In a new version, especially for a barn, the large pan which contains the apples is placed on the floor just beyond the end of a small rug. As the victim is trying to catch the apples the rug is pulled from under him, dunking his face in the water. Pick a good sport for this one.

(2) *Guessing games.* Here are some suggestions to use for guessing games:

1. How many pins in a paper of pins?
2. How many beans in a quart measure?
3. How many peanuts in a glass jar?
4. How many pumpkin seeds in a cup?
5. How many grains of corn in a glass tumbler?

Let the players look at the items you have prepared for several seconds.

(3) *Hallowe'en sounds.* After the leader has been hidden behind a screen with his necessary tools and props, the teenagers are given paper and pencil on which to write their guesses of the noises which he will make. The following list is suggested:
1. Sawing wood
2. Eating celery
3. Winding a clock
4. Breaking a dish
5. Striking a match
6. Driving a nail
7. Rattling a baby rattle
8. Cracking nuts
9. Turning pages of a newspaper
10. Sweeping with a broom
11. Cutting open a pumpkin
12. Eating an apple
13. Pouring cider from one glass to another

(4) *Mirror contest.* One at a time the boys and girls sit before a mirror and the leader holds a milk bottle over the contestant's head. At the side is a can of peanuts. The contestant looks only at the mirror as he picks up the peanuts and drops them into the bottle one at a time. The one who can drop the most into a bottle in two minutes wins a prize.

(5) *Block heads.* After all of the costumes have been judged and the masks have been removed, an interesting Hallowe'en game may be played with paper sacks. A numbered slip, a card, a pencil and a large paper bag are given to each guest. He pins the slip on his chest, then tears eye holes in the sack, slips it over his head and goes forth among the teenagers to try to recognize as many of the other guests as possible, writing their numbers and names on his card. Each person will endeavor to keep himself anonymous.

(6) *Ghosts alive!* While the boys are out of the room the girls are seated on chairs and each is completely covered with a sheet. When the boys return each young man stands in front of a different ghost and begins the process of trying to identify the girl. He may ask the ghost to groan, boo, hiss, meow, whistle, cough, bark, sigh, or make any other sound, but not speak any words. The process continues until each boy has identified a ghost. If the game seems to be a lot of fun it may be repeated.

(7) *Ghost and broom.* Players stand in a circle facing in with their hands behind them. One player is given the "Ghost" which is a large white handkerchief tied to resemble a ghost. Blindfold a player who is *It*. Stand *It* in the middle of the circle and give him a broom. When *It* raps once on the floor with the broom, the Ghost is passed about the circle, each player taking it in turn. When *It* raps again with the broom the passing stops, and *It* tries to guess who has the Ghost. If a guess is right, that player changes places with *It* and the game continues. If the guess was not correct, passing continues and other guesses are made.

(8) *Fido's dinner.* Place a doughnut on a paper place mat on the floor before each of the boys. At the signal, ask them to eat the doughnut without touching it with his hands. The one who finishes his doughnut first is the winner. This will be the beginning of refreshment time for the boys.

Refreshments

Doughnuts
Apples   Popcorn
Potato chips
Hot chocolate or cold cider

Devotions

One of the saddest and most gruesome stories in the Old Testament is the narrative concerning Saul and his failure as a king. He became jealous when he heard the people on the streets singing their praises to David who had slain Goliath. Filled with a jealous rage he endeavored to kill David with a javelin but failed. He spent the rest of his life in fiendish expressions of jealousy which finally led him to a state of depression which resulted in a visit to the witch of Endor and eventual suicide. The story is found in I Samuel 28:7.

CHRISTMAS CAROL PARTY

Junior High youngsters have reached the age when they enjoy dressing up to go to a party. There is no better time for this than Christmas. A happy but dignified party may be built around the theme of the Christmas carols. This can even be made into a dinner party.

Decorations

Any of the traditional home decorations for Christmas will be suitable for the Junior High Carol party. As much as possible, use decorations which emphasize the spiritual aspect of the Christmas season. Large cutouts of Christmas figures are especially desirable. A Christmas manger scene and a Christmas tree are always appropriate.

Things to Do

(1) *Records.* Many Christmas records are available which have been planned for group participation. Not all the songs on every record, however, are appropriate. Help may be received from your local Christian supply center. Also, there are many Christmas records which can be enjoyed by the group while they sit and visit with each other. Each teenager may be asked to bring his own favorite Christmas record.

(2) *Pantomime or charades.* An old stand-by for Junior High entertainment is the pantomime or charade. Adapt these to the titles of Christmas carols. Below is a suggested list:
"It Came Upon the Midnight Clear"
"Angels From the Realms of Glory"
"Silent Night, Holy Night"
"O Come All Ye Faithful"
"Sweet Little Jesus Boy"

(3) *Game centers.* Provide three game centers which may be used immediately as the young people arrive. Provide the types of games which several children can play at once. Suggestions include pick-up-sticks, spinning games, ring toss, and puzzles.

(4) *Poinsettia relay.* Secure two long-stemmed artificial poinsettia. Place each in a vase some distance from the starting line. Each person in line must go to the vase, take out the poinsettia and bring it to the second in line. The second in line must take the flower back to its place in the vase, and return to touch the hand of the next in line who once more goes after the flower. After every person on the team has run the course, the flower must be finally taken back to its original place in the vase. The first team finished wins.

(5) *Make decorations.* Christmas bells may be made from egg cartons. Use the type of egg carton which nests the egg in solid pressed paper. Break or cut loose each individual egg cup and trim edges evenly

to form bell shape. Spray bells with gold paint. For single bell, make clapper of metallic paper. Fasten clapper at center of bell with heavy thread. Put thread through cup at center and make loop at end of thread to serve as hanger. For multiple string, finish first bell with clapper, then fasten plain bells above it at even intervals, first knotting thread to hold bell in place. Three or five bells make the best proportioned strings. Decorate bells with painted or pasted-on stars.

A Christmas paper chain can be made for excellent tree decoration. This basic bit of tree ornament can be as gay as a string of tinsel but very inexpensive. In its simplest form it is interlocking rings or links of plain paper heavy enough to hold a round shape. A one inch by five inch strip makes a nice flat loop. Metallic paper with white inside for contrast makes a fancy chain. For a still more fancy chain, scallop the edges of the strips. Fold a five inch strip once in center, making ends meet. Fold twice again but with folds only ¼ inch from end, then cut on curved line. The quarter inch allowance is for joining and keeping scallops open. An old pair of pinking shears will give fancy saw tooth edges. For multi colored effect, use a variety of papers.

(6) *Christmas stories.* Junior High children can enjoy participating in the telling of stories if they have been given advance notice. Library copies are available on these old classic Christmas stories:

1. *Why the Chimes Rang* by Raymond MacDonald Alden
2. *A Christmas Carol* by Charles Dickens
3. *The Gift of the Magi* by O. Henry
4. *The Christmas Angel* by Henry Van Dyke

(7) *Caroling.* While refreshments are being prepared the group may do some Christmas caroling in the neighborhood.

Refreshments

Assorted finger sandwiches
Fruited gelatin with whipped cream
Decorated cup cakes
Hot chocolate

Devotions

Suggest that since several beautiful Christmas stories have been told, it is appropriate to conclude the party with the telling of the greatest Christmas story of all. You may then read or tell the story of Luke, chapter two. Or it may be fitting in some groups to read a brief chapter on the birth of Jesus as told in Fulton Oursler's *The Greatest Story Ever Told,* which is available in all libraries.

APRIL FOOL'S DAY BACKWARD PARTY

Your "tweenagers" may cut all the capers they like at this party. Everything possible is done the wrong way around. Costumes are worn inside out, wrong side front, and even upside down. The guests are received at the back door instead of the front door. The invitation is written backward and upside down so it has to be read in a mirror. Boys may sit on chairs backwards, wear shoes with the toes poked into the heels, shake hands with the left hand calling to everyone, "Goodbye, I had a nice time," as they enter.

Decorations

Over the door where the young people enter, write the word "exit." The color scheme for the decorations may be black and white. White table covering; black paper napkins; black place cards with white dunce caps upside down, and the names printed backward in white ink. Place a dunce hat over a large bowl in the center of the table. From each plate run a black ribbon streamer to the bowl. Tie on various favors such as whistles, puzzles and trick gadgets. The table is set to accommodate left-handed persons. Forks are on the right, tumblers on the left, etc. Serve the refreshments when the group first arrives. A good refreshment for this party is upside-down cake.

Things to Do

(1) *Backward spelling bee*. In this kind of spelling bee all the words are spelled backwards. If the word is correctly spelled backwards the speller stays in his place. If he incorrectly spells it backwards, he sits down. The one left standing last is the winner. Below is a suggested list of only one dozen words which may be a challenge to spell backwards. You will need to extend this list to accommodate the number of your guests:

    cat
    dog
    street
    cap
    nut
    hat
    wood
    ball
    jar
    auto
    mush
    slap

(2) *Guessing game*. There are many ways to adapt the idea of the guessing game to an April Fool's theme. Here are some suggestions:
1. Guess the number of nuts contained in a large dunce cap
2. Guess the weight of an egg
3. Guess the number of toothpicks in a saucepan

(3) *Talkfest*. Two players talk

fast and furiously for thirty seconds on any subject they choose or a subject suggested by the leader. Variations include singing, recitation of the alphabet, and reciting the books of the Bible. Also, the game may be changed by asking three people to talk on the same subject for as long as they can. Let the group vote for the best "talker."

(4) *Waiter.* This little game provides fun for the spectators and players. The only gear required is a paper plate nine inches in diameter and three small rubber balls about one or one-and-a-half inches in diameter for each player. Styrofoam balls may be used instead of rubber ones.

Each player stands beside his starting marker and holds his tray and the three balls. On the word "go" each player becomes a waiter. He places the balls in the tray and races to the opposite marker holding the tray level with his head and balanced on three fingers and thumb of his hand.

* See Party Recipes section in back of book.

When he reaches the second marker the waiter changes the tray from one hand to the other and races back to the starting point with his tray still balanced above his head. Should one or more balls roll from the tray at any point, the waiter has to stop, place the tray on the ground, replace the fallen balls and continue as before.

(5) *Backward film.* An exciting time may be had by the entire group if a good sports or travelog film is shown backwards. The result is hilarious.

Refreshments
Pineapple upside-down cake*
Cold milk served in
half-pint cartons

Devotions

The party may be closed on a fairly serious note by reading the final paragraph in the last book of the Bible. This invitation in the Word is easily turned to evangelism, even at an April Fool's party.

AN ALL-DAY PARTY FOR 'TWEENAGERS'

There are certain times of the year when it is good for the entire youth group of the church to spend a full day and evening together. Such times as Friday after Thanksgiving, New Year's Day, Spring vacations, the day after Christmas and other off-party times work out nicely. The idea of entertaining the young people for such a long period need not be frightening if plenty of advance planning is done.

Decorations

No decorations are really necessary, unless there is to be a centerpiece on the table at night. Even so, this should be planned by the young people themselves and included with their do it-yourself meal. Leave this to their own imagination.

Things to Do

9 A.M. to 11 A.M.. *Work shift.* Find some project to which the young people can give their energies for the first two hours of the day. This might include a cleaning project at the church, mowing the grass for an elderly couple, hauling firewood, or any other thing that would do the performance of a good deed.

11 A.M. to 12 noon. *Game time.* Provide a number of parlor games and sports which young people enjoy. They can entertain themselves in small or large groups with such games as Monoply, Anagrams, ping pong, basketball, or volleyball.

12 noon to 1 P.M. *Lunch.* This should be a sack lunch provided by each person. The sponsor can provide cokes or other drinks for the group. If the group is too large to be seated around a table, they may spread their lunch on the floor.

1 P.M. to 3 P.M. *Recreational activity.* During this time slot, plan for the young folks to take an educational excursion to such places as museums, business enterprises, art galleries, or public buildings.

3. P.M. to 5 P.M. *Game time.* This will be a continuation of the free time provided for games prior to lunch. If a few games are available to the young people they will have no trouble in entertaining themselves.

5 P.M. to 7 P.M. *Do-it-yourself-dinner.* Let each of the young people get involved in the preparation for the evening meal. It may be organized around 1) table setting, 2) decorations, 3) salads, 4) main dish, 5) desserts, 6) clean up.

7 P.M. to 10 P.M. *Activity time.* The day may be ended by informal play or discussion time in the home, or by attendance at a sports or church event.

Do-It-Yourself-Menu

This menu should be planned by the group. Their ideas of the meal should be used to make it a complete do-it-yourself dinner.

Devotions

Assign each of the young people one of the three parables in the fifteenth chapter of the Gospel according to St. Luke. Ask each to read his parable and then tell what it means to him:

1. parable of the lost sheep
2. parable of the lost coin
3. parable of the lost boy

A CANDY KITCHEN PARTY

Junior High young people will get special enjoyment out of a well-planned party which features the making of homemade candy. Some of the better types of candy to be made on this occasion include chocolate fudge, pralines, caramel corn, and caramel apples.

Decorations

No decorations in the traditional sense are needed for this party. However, it will help considerably if every young person present is given a chef's type hat and a large apron to wear. In fact, each one can be asked to bring his own cap and apron.

Things to Do

1. *Recipe for chocolate fudge.*
Place the following ingredients in a large bowl and set aside:
1 package chocolate chips
1 cup chopped nuts
¼ lb. butter
1 teaspoon vanilla
Boil the following in a heavy sauce pan for six minutes, stirring constantly:
2 cups sugar
¾ cup condensed milk
10 large marshmallows
 (may be cut)
After boiling six minutes pour hot mixture over other ingredients. Stir until chocolate chips and butter are melted. Pour on greased platter.

2. *Recipe for pralines.*
1½ cup sugar
½ cup brown sugar
1 tablespoon butter
½ cup evaporated milk
1 package butterscotch pudding
Pecans
Cook three to five minutes until soft ball stage. Pour on greased foil. Cut in squares.

3. *Recipe for caramel corn.*
8 cups popcorn
½ cup dark corn syrup
½ cup sugar
½ teaspoon salt
Place popcorn in a large kettle over medium heat. Mix together dark corn syrup, sugar and salt. Add to popcorn in kettle and stir constantly over medium heat three to five minutes, until corn is completely coated with mixture. Remove from heat. Spread on waxed paper and separate the pieces of popcorn.

4. *Recipe for caramel apples.*
3 cups sugar
Few grains salt
1 cup corn syrup
2⅔ cups evaporated milk
Small apples
Place sugar, salt, syrup and ⅔ cup milk in large kettle. Stir to blend and heat slowly until sugar is melted. Boil rapidly until mixture is thick. Stir in remainder of milk slowly, keep-

ing mixture at a boil. Boil to firm ball stage, 242 degrees. Apples should be room temperature and should be washed and well dried. Stick the apples on wooden skewers. Dip apples in caramel mixture, one at a time. Whirl in pan to remove excess caramel. Place with handle end up on a well-greased platter. If coating becomes hard, reheat or put coating over pan of hot water while dipping apples. Coating should be kept hot.

Refreshments

In addition to the candy being made by the teenagers, there should be an ample supply of cold milk, and perhaps some cheese and crackers which will offset the sweetness of the candy.

Devotions

Ask one of the teenagers to read Psalm 51 and comment on each of the promises David made to God for the forgiveness and cleansing of his sin.

INDOOR PICNIC PARTY

This party must be planned in a gymnasium or other large room. The games will all be active. At refreshment time everyone will be seated on blankets on the floor and refreshments served picnic style.

Decorations

Build a booth with red and white bunting which may look like a Fourth of July fire-cracker stand. This will be the place from which prizes are given out and also where the young people may come for cold drinks which are provided.

Things to Do

(1) *Nail driving contest.*

(2) *Sack race.*

(3) *Three-legged race.*

(4) *Tag games.*

(5) *Basketball free throw contest.*

(6) *Bean bag toss.*

(7) *Relay races.*

(8) Any other games of skill which may be adapted to the space where the party is held.

Refreshments

Fried chicken
Potato salad   Rolls
Pickles — olives
Cake
Cold drinks

Devotions

In a letter St. Paul sent to his young friend Timothy he included this bit of advice, "Bodily exercise profiteth little, but righteousness exalteth the man." Ask the supervisor or even the Pastor to bring a three- or four-minute sermonette on this verse of Scripture, perhaps based on the following outline:

1. St. Paul seems to have been much interested in athletics. This is based on his many references to athletic terms such as the race, wrestling, crowns for the winners, and training weights.

2. There is good which comes from bodily exercise. Every person must take good care of his body because it is the temple of the Holy Spirit.

3. The most profitable exercise is spiritual. Spiritual exercise consists of obedience, faith, and Christian service.

A LANTERN HIKE PARTY

All of the teenagers are asked to bring lanterns with them to the party if possible. The lanterns will be carried by the young folks as they hike to the spot where the party is to be held. Having arrived at the outdoor clearing where the party will continue, the lanterns are either hung from tree limbs or placed on forked sticks driven into the ground. The more lanterns the better.

Decorations

Except for the lanterns, the only other decorations needed will be an open fire. It may be helpful to provide some logs or camp stools for seating if the ground tends to be damp.

Things to Do

(1) *Hike*. The hike should be planned for a long distance but not more than the young folks can handle without fatigue. If possible, plan the hike on a night of the full moon.

(2) *Candle race*. In this race each runner carries a lighted candle. If a candle snuffs out, the player must go back and start over again. This may be done as a relay and cause considerable hilarity.

(3) *Charades*. Suitable subjects for campfire charades may include the following: 1) "S.O.S." 2) "Come-and-get-it" 3) "Hit the sack" 4) "Up and at 'em."

(4) *Song time*. Here are some of the campfire favorites:
"There's a Long, Long Trail."
"Let the Lower Lights Be Burning."
"Standing Somewhere in the Shadows."
"Church in the Wildwood."

(5) *Testimony time*. Prepare a stack of small sticks of wood which have been dipped in a flammable material. As each person begins his testimony, one of these is tossed onto the fire causing a momentary increase to the blaze.

Refreshments

Weiner roast at the campfire
Corn chips
Somores *
Kool-aid

Devotions

Tell the story of St. Paul's shipwreck on the Island of Malta. This story in the Book of Acts can be the introduction of the passage of Scripture concerning Paul's experience at the campfire. Acts 28:2.

1. Fire may stir the memory of past experiences.
2. Fire reminds us of the cleansing power of the Holy Spirit.
3. Fire may remind us of the need for continued devotional living.

* See Party Recipes section in back of book.

DOCTOR'S FUN CLINIC

Not every group will be interested in this type of party. However, an interesting social time can be built around the medical theme. If not used for a full scale party, this idea may well be adapted for an after-church hearth-side or fellowship hour for Junior High young people.

Decorations

Decorate the meeting room as a clinic or doctor's office using wall charts, bottles, hospital equipment, and even a wheel chair. The actual atmosphere of a physician's office may be created by using a heavy amount of medicinal-smelling room spray.

Things to Do

(1) *Name tags.* Give everyone a special name for the evening. This name should be pinned on a large card attached to the lapel or shoulder. Some names may be Dr. Curall, Dr. Quack, and Dr. Bone.

(2) *Steady nerves.* Teams may compete on the steadiness of their nerves. They may do this by seeing who can stand on one foot the longest. Also, a relay race may be played by asking each team to thread a needle. Or, they may contend to see who can balance a ball the longest.

(3) *Calisthenics.* This is a variation of the game "Simon Says." The leader asks everyone to do what the doctor says. If the doctor says "Bend," they bend. If the doctor says, "Jump," they jump. However, if the leader does some calisthenic exercise without first using the words, "Doctor says," then none of the others are to obey him. Anyone who does obey him drops out. The last one standing is the winner.

(4) *Capsule program.* Large empty capsules may be secured from a veterinary or possibly a hospital supply house. These capsules may be filled with pieces of paper which give program suggestions. Every person is given a capsule and as each one opens his, he must do whatever the paper says. Of course, it will be up to the leader to see that certain people with special gifts receive the right capsule containing the best instructions for them.

The Diet

Chicken broth
Crackers
Plain Jello or custard
Vanila wafers
Weak tea

Devotions

Dr. Luke was the Great physician who accompanied Paul on many of his journeys. The narrative in the Book of Acts changes from "they" to "we" in the story of events at Troas (Acts 16:6-11). One commentator indicates Luke probably was a ship's doctor because of his evident knowledge of the sea (Acts 27). Another writer even suggests he may have been a student with Paul (Saul) in the University at Tarsus. At any rate the Scriptures contain three revealing characteristics about him:

1. Colossians 4:14, "Luke the beloved physician."
2. Philemon verse 24: "Luke my fellow worker."
3. II Timothy 4:9-11, "Only Luke is with me."

GIRLS' PAJAMA PARTY

This is a favorite with fourteen- and fifteen-year-old girls. Four or five girls are invited to come for dinner and to spend the night. There must be an assortment of snack foods on hand such as: milk, fruit juices, cold drinks, cheese dips, potato chips, pretzels, cookies, tarts, brownies, cupcakes, ice cream from the freezer, candy, and nuts. (Pistachio nuts are especially fun.)

Decorations

The only decoration needed for a pajama party is a well-vacuumed house. Clean sheets, lots of beds, fresh towels, an efficient television set, and plenty of records will complete the needed equipment.

Things to Do

(1) *Write letters.* Provide paper, envelopes, stamps, and ball point pens for each girl to write a letter to someone. Perhaps all the girls could write to one special person.

(2) *Fun in the kitchen.* Some girls may be interested in trying favorite recipes to serve the group.

(3) *Free time.* Much of the evening and night will be happily used by the girls in conversation.

(4) *Records and television.* The girls may entertain themselves with their favorite records and television programs.

Refreshments

For the dinner hour as the guests arrive, plan a spaghetti supper. Serve meat sauce over spaghetti. Pass parmesan cheese. Accompany with a tossed green salad and garlic French bread. Serve ice cold milk and omit a dessert.

Devotions

Plan devotions around a lengthy reading of some particular passage in the Bible. If there are five girls present, it may be well to have each of the girls read one of the chapters in the letter of St. James. If there are four girls, they may read the book of Philippians; etc.

SCHOOLHOUSE PARTY

This party is particularly good for the September schedule or for the period immediately after Christmas vacation. Although many Junior High young people may profess to dislike school, they will have the time of their lives mimicking the ideas of learning in a fun evening.

Decorations

On large sheets of paper, scrawl notes to the teacher which can be pinned to the curtain for decorations. Perhaps a blackboard may be secured to fasten to the wall or to be placed on a tripod at one end of the room. A table may be decorated with a stack of books bound together with a leather strap. Place an apple for the teacher on top of the books. Use of globes and maps will help to further carry out the schoolroom idea.

Things to Do

(1) *Portrait sketching.* Give each person pencil and paper. Ask each player to draw part of a portrait, then fold that portion of the paper under and pass it on to the next person who adds to the portrait and folds under his portion, passing it along to another. When about four persons have worked on one portrait, it may be opened and displayed.

(2) *Arithmetic stunt.* Count the number of guests present and announce it to the group. Then direct them to get into groups of the stated size. For instance, you may say, "Mix in fives." When the groups are all of the same number, then ask them to mix in groups of another number. When you call out, "Mix in tens," it really gets confusing.

(3) *Bible names.* There are three methods for using this game as follows:

1. Mimeograph copies of the contest and have guests fill in the correct names.
2. Call out the symbols and ask the guests to shout the answers either as individuals or as a group.
3. Display objects or pictures representing the symbols. Ask the guests to move along the line of symbols, identifying the objects on their sheet of paper. The following symbols and characters are suggested as a beginning for your longer list which will be adapted to the number and Bible understanding of your group.

1) A rainbow (Noah)
2) A slingshot (David)
3) A coat of many colors (Joseph)
4) Long hair (Samson)
5) A big fisherman (Peter)
6) A bag of money (Judas)
7) An alabaster box (Mary)
8) A rod (Moses)

(4) *Bible alphabet.* Ask everyone to make a list in one column of the entire alphabet. Then ask each person to go back and write in a Bible name of a person, place or thing which begins with each letter of the alphabet. This is more difficult than it may seem at first glance.

(5) *Counseling session.* Give each person two small cards, one yellow and one white. (Any other two colors may be chosen.) Ask each person to write a question on the white card and a foolish answer to it on the yellow card. Collect the cards and mix up questions and answers before redistributing them to the group. Every person must read the question and then the answer which he has drawn.

(6) *Observation test.* A tray with six to ten familiar articles on it is shown to the young people. When it is taken away, each one tries to recall everything that was there by writing the list of objects on their paper.

(7) *Spell my name.* This is a version of the old-fashioned spelling bee. Divide the group into two teams and see who can remain standing the longest by spelling the names of Bible characters. The following list is a good starter:

Adam	Goliath	Philip
Eve	Hannah	Rachel
Enoch	Herod	Reuben
Noah	Isaac	Samuel
Ham	Isaiah	Saul
Shem	Jacob	Simeon
Japheth	Jeremiah	Solomon
Cain	Jezebel	Stephen
Caleb	Job	Thomas
Daniel	Joshua	Titus
Delilah	Lazarus	Timothy
Dorcas	Levi	Uz
Elijah	Matthew	Esther
Elisha	Miriam	Moses
Felix	Nathan	Luke
Gabriel	Naomi	Zebedee
Gideon	Pilate	

(8) *Bible hunt.* Divide your group into two teams. Provide two large maps of Bible lands. Mention a particular place and let each group compete against the other to find the place on the map first.

Refreshments

Provide each guest with a school lunch. For each sack: peanut butter sandwich or bologna sandwich, a red apple, assorted cookies, a small candy bar and a napkin. Secure small cartons of orange drink from the dairy. Provide straws.

Devotions

A wonderful suggestion was made by St. Paul to a young friend of his when he said, "Study to show thyself approved unto God, a workman that needeth not to be ashamed, rightly dividing the word of truth" (II Timothy 2:15). There are several applications which may be made from this verse. Some suggestions are as follows:

1. The importance of study both at school and at Sunday school.
2. Our primary goal is to be approved of God.
3. It is not needful for God's workmen to be ashamed in their knowledge and use of the Bible.
4. Truth can never really become meaningful to any individual until he grasps it for himself. We can only explain the truth to others when we understand it ourselves.

A BANKER'S PARTY

Junior High young people are just beginning to understand the power of their own money. Many of them are on allowances, have their first part-time jobs, and are concerned about the things they can buy. It is likely all of them will enjoy a party built around the theme of money.

Decorations

Go to your local savings and loans companies to see what out-sized coins and dollar bills they have available which can be used for your party decorations. A centerpiece may be made by beginning with a piggy bank. Surround it with chocolate foil-covered coins. Give everyone a bag of the candy coins as a party favor.

Things to Do

(1) *Investment money.* Give each guest $50.00 in play money for use during the course of the evening. Then announce that the forbidden word for the evening is "money." Each time a person uses the word "money" they must give up a dollar bill to the person who has caught them saying it. At the end of the evening give a prize to the person who has the most play money. Give a box of dollar mints as the prize.

(2) *Name tags.* Use a felt pen to write names on play money. Pin identifying bill to the lapel of each guest.

(3) *Penny guess.* Fill a quart jar with pennies and ask the group to guess how many are in it.

(4) *Know your money.* See how many can tell you the names of persons whose pictures appear on the various issues of paper currency.

$1.00	Washington
$2.00	Jefferson
$5.00	Lincoln
$10.00	Hamilton
$20.00	Jackson
$50.00	Grant
$100.00	Franklin
$500.00	McKinley
$1,000.00	Cleveland
$10,000.00	Chase

(5) *Hidden numbers.* Place a series of small cards around the room in plain sight but so located that the color of each closely matches the background color where it is placed. The cards on which the numbers are written are in plain sight but difficult to see. Distribute paper and pencils to the teenagers. Ask each person to write his name on the sheet of paper and then wander around the room trying to locate all the numbers he or she can find. Set the time limit of ten minutes and instruct the guests not to touch the numbers or talk

about them. The guest finding the most wins the prize.

Refreshments

Lettuce sandwiches
Chocolate fudge squares*
Whipped cream
Lemonade

* See Party Recipes section in back of book.

Devotions

Jesus had much to say about money. Not the least of His sayings on the subject are recorded in the Sermon on the Mount — Matthew 6:1-4; Matthew 6:19; Matthew 6:25; Matthew 6:33.

MISSIONARY FURLOUGH PARTY

Many young people have a mistaken idea that missionaries must be very somber people who have little sense of humor. While there is a missionary on furlough in your area, plan a party of the Junior High young folks with the missionary as honored guest. It will be good for the young people and the missionary.

Decorations

Japanese lanterns, Indian saris, or Spanish shawls may be used according to the locale in which the missionary has served. Also, travel posters are almost always available from local travel agencies.

Things to Do

(1) *Sock race.* A sock race is run with each contestant holding unto the tops of both his socks. This can be adapted well as a relay.

(2) *Pantomime suggestions.*
1. A girl rolling up her hair.
2. A ball player striking out with the bases full.
3. A catcher after a high foul.
4. A beggar pan-handling.
5. A mechanical doll walking.
6. A poor golfer trying to tee off.
7. A drum major strutting.
8. A concert pianist.

Divide all the guests into groups of no more than four or five. Let each group choose their own pantomime subject. Let the group vote for the best performed pantomime.

(3) *Who has gone?* The young people stand or sit in a circle. One player is *It*. He closes his eyes and puts his hands over them. The leader motions for some player to leave the room. That player does so quietly. The player who is *It* then opens his eyes and tries to guess which person has left the room. If he guesses correctly the player who went out becomes *It*. If not, *It* continues until he does guess correctly.

(4) *Who am I?* Cut out pictures of well-known persons and celebrities from magazines and newspapers. As the guests arrive, pin one on the back of each person. Everyone then tries to find out who has been pinned on his back. He may ask questions of the others who look to see who he is and then answer his questions by saying "yes" or "no."

(5) *The glad hand.* This is good to use for pairing off the group to receive refreshments. Make as many pairs of hands from colored paper as there are guests at your party. The hands should be different in size and shape but there should be two alike of each type. Use one of the sets of hands to distribute to the boys and the other to the girls. Each boy must search out among the girls to find the person who has a hand matching his.

She becomes his partner for refreshments.

(6) *Missionary pictures*. If a missionary is willing, the last portion of the party may become more serious as pictures of the mission field are shown in either slides or movies.

Refreshments

If possible, try to prepare some refreshment dish which is at least a reminder of the area from which the missionary has come. The missionary may be able to guide you on this.

Devotions

Ask the missionary to conclude the party with a few comments on the subject, "How Can Young People Know a Call to Full-time Christian Service?"

GYMNASIUM PARTY

Junior High young folks are very active. Parties planned to absorb their great amounts of energy are usually popular. If you have a large party room or better still a gymnasium in the church, a wonderful evening can be planned several times a year which will prove to be a highlight on the Junior High social calendar.

Decorations

Several small tables which are planned for holding various snack foods may be decorated with bright cloths and crepe paper streamers. On one table provide a huge bowl of popcorn. On another, place an ample supply of potato chips with several kinds of dip young people like. On another table place a good supply of apples and/or other fruit. One table should have cold drinks. A final table may be used for placing any parlor games which are not being played by one of the groups. The activities will be planned in such an informal manner that several different types of party things may be going on simultaneously. However, the tables will always be the centers of interest.

Things to Do

(1) *Parlor games.* Ask everyone to bring one or two of their favorite games including dominoes, checkers, chinese checkers, and Scrabble.

(2) *Gymnasium games.* If facilities are available, plan opportunities to play ping pong, volleyball, and even basketball.

(3) *Free time.* Around a fireplace or other center of interest, provide chairs for relaxed conversation by persons who may not, at least momentarily, be interested in any of the games.

(4) *Marshmallow delight.* The boys and girls who enter this contest are due for a big surprise, and a laugh too. The game is announced as just another eating contest in which the girl feeds the boy four marshmallows and then he in turn feeds the girl four marshmallows. The first couple to finish all their marshmallows wins. However, the players are blindfolded and then given the marshmallows in paper bags. They should not be allowed to see the bags before being blindfolded. Each marshmallow should have been coated with charcoal dust before the game. Players will unwittingly make black marks on each other's faces as they try to feed the marshmallows to one another. Spectators will be watching the black streaks develop.

(5) *Nail-driving championship.* A wooden block made by nailing together short lengths of two-inch pine planks is needed. Also eight-penny nails are needed. This is a good

early bird contest, something to amuse the people who arrive before the regular party time begins. The object of the game is to see which person can drive a nail in up to its head with the fewest number of hammer blows. The contestants are given one eight-penny nail about two and one-half inches long. All contestants use the same hammer. A judge should count every blow including the first blow that starts the nail into the wood. If a nail is bent over, and many are, he must count the number of taps given to straighten it. After the boys have had a good round of nail-driving, allow the girls to compete among each other.

(6) *A weight-guessing contest.* Choose a half-dozen of your guests to be weighed after all the guests have attempted to guess their weight. A set of bathroom scales will do to weigh each of the six people. Give some high calorie prize such as a bag of chocolates to the person who is most successful at guessing the weights.

(7) *Rolling contest.* Fasten a line of white tape across the floor about eight feet from and parallel to the wall. As many contestants as the width of the room will permit line up in back of this line. Each is given a tennis ball. The object of the game is to roll the ball against the baseboard of the opposite wall so it will return to the tape line. The contestant whose ball stops rolling closest to the tape is declared the winner.

(8) *The bouncing ball.* Place a wastebasket on the floor and, two or three feet in front of it, place a kitchen chair with its back away from the basket. Each contestant in turn stands about eight feet away from the back of the chair and tries to bounce a tennis ball on the floor between himself and the chair so it will go over the chair and land in the wastebasket. Each player is given three turns in succession. Ten points are given for each basket made and the game is won with a total of one hundred points.

(9) *Paper bag relay race.* Appoint two leaders who take turns in choosing their team. Teams line up to mark and paper bags are placed on two chairs about twenty feet away. At the signal to start, the first in each line runs to the chair, blows up a bag, pops it, runs back and tags the next in line who then repeats the performance. If desired, a small prize may be awarded to each member of the winning team.

Refreshments

Hamburgers with lots of trimmings
Cokes

Devotions

Use Hebrews chapter twelve, verses one and two for the closing devotions. Lessons may be as follows:
1. In the game of life we are conconstantly being watched.
2. In the game of life there is great need for training and self-discipline.
3. No one wins in the game of life who does not develop patience.
4. Jesus must be considered as both the Starter and the Finisher of the race.

PARTY RECIPES
(A few favorites)

Banana Boat Plate

Place a banana on a "sea" of lettuce leaves. Cut a sail out of blue construction paper and attach with a long plastic toothpick. Decorate boat with whipped cream, raisins, peanuts and cherries. Make a gangplank out of a fresh or canned pineapple spear. Prepare an individual banana boat plate for each guest.

Cambric Tea

Cambric tea is a weak tea to which is added about an equal amount of hot milk, plus sugar to taste. It is usually accepted by children as a most satisfactory substitute for the adult drink.

Chicken Loaf

1 chicken, cooked tender
2 cups soft bread crumbs
1 cup cooked rice
1 tablespoon salt
1 teaspoon paprika
¼ cup chopped pimento
4 eggs, well beaten
¼ cup butter
¾ quart chicken stock

Remove chicken from bone and dice. Combine all ingredients in order given and mix well. Pack into flat baking dish. Bake in a slow oven until set like custard. Allow to stand ten minutes in pan before serving. Serve with the following sauce.

¼ cup butter
¼ cup flour
2 cups chicken stock

Melt butter in saucepan. Stir in flour. Add liquid and continue stirring until smooth.

Add:
1 can mushrooms
2 beaten egg yolks
¼ cup cream

Also add salt, paprika, chopped parsley and one teaspoon lemon juice.

Chocolate Fudge Squares

½ pound vanilla wafers, crushed
1 cup chopped nuts
⅔ cup butter
1 cup powdered sugar

3 eggs, separated
1½ squares chocolate, melted
½ teaspoon vanilla
1 cup whipping cream, whipped

Mix the crushed wafers and chopped nuts with one-third cup of the butter, which has been melted. Use one-half of this mixture to cover the bottom and sides of a nine-inch square pan. Cream the remaining butter and sugar together. Add the well-beaten egg yolks, the melted chocolate and the vanilla. Fold in the stiffly beaten egg whites. Pour into the crumb-lined pan and spread the remaining nuts and crumbs over the top. Let stand in the refrigerator overnight. Cut and serve in three-inch squares. Serve with whipped cream. Serves nine.

Corn Bread Muffins

⅓ cup shortening
⅓ cup sugar
1 egg, beaten
1¼ cups milk

1 cup flour
½ teaspoon salt
4 teaspoons baking powder
1 cup yellow corn meal

Cream shortening and sugar. Add egg and milk. Sift together flour, salt and baking powder and add to shortening mixture. Add corn meal, stirring just enough to mix. Fill geased muffin tins two-thirds full; bake in hot oven (425 degrees) for about 25 minutes. (Yield: one dozen.)

Delicious May Baskets

Bake cupcakes in fluted paper cups of pastel colors. Frost cakes and decorate with frosting flowers. Make the handle of the "basket" with pipe cleaner, securing to the paper cup with scotch tape. Tie a small ribbon bow on each handle. Serve on small paper doilies.

Doll Cake

Bake a packaged white or yellow cake in a mixing bowl. When cool, insert a tall doll in the center. The doll should be exposed from the waist up. With cake decorator, form a lovely frosting dress for the doll. On the skirt, which is the cake, make many rows of frosting ruffles and add small bows or flower decorations.

Fruit Tea

2 quarts water
½ teaspoon whole cloves
¼ teaspoon allspice
Juice of 2 oranges

¼ cup lemon juice
¾ cup sugar
1 small tea bag (black tea)

Boil water, fruit juices, sugar and spices together for fifteen minutes. Turn off heat and add tea bag. Let stand fifteen minutes and pour through strainer. Reheat just before serving. Serves sixteen.

Pineapple Upside-Down Cake

2 egg yolks
¾ cup sugar
¼ cup hot pineapple syrup
¾ cup cake flour
Pinch of salt
½ teaspoon baking powder
½ teaspoon vanilla
2 stiffly beaten egg whites

Beat egg yolks until very thick; add sugar and continue beating. Add syrup; mix well and add sifted ingredients. Mix until smooth. Add vanilla. Fold in beaten egg whites. Pour over the following which has been prepared in an eight-inch square cake pan:

¼ cup melted butter
⅔ cup brown sugar

Over this arrange nine pineapple slices. Place a maraschino cherry in the center of each ring. Pour batter over. Bake at 325° about one hour.

Somores

Toast marshmallows and place between graham crackers. Also, put a square of Hershey's chocolate candy bar in each sandwich. The toasted marshmallow will tend to melt the chocolate bar and hold the ingredients together. It is said the treat received this name because when you taste one you want "some more."

Teddy Bear or Gingerbread Boy Cookies

⅔ cup shortening
1 cup sugar
1 egg, beaten
¼ cup molasses, light
2 cups flour
1 teaspoon soda
1 teaspoon salt
1 teaspoon ginger
1 teaspoon cinnamon
½ teaspoon ground cloves

Cream shortening and sugar thoroughly. Add egg and molasses and beat well. Add sifted dry ingredients and mix well. Roll dough one-eighth inch thick on lightly floured board. Cut with teddy bear cookie cutter or gingerbread boy cutter. Bake on greased cookie sheet in 350° oven about ten minutes. (Yield: 6 dozen cookies.)